THE $1 MILLION
REASON TO
CHANGE
YOUR MIND

Pat Mesiti

Wrightbooks

First published 2009 by Wrightbooks
an imprint of John Wiley & Sons Australia, Ltd
42 McDougall St, Milton Qld 4064

Office also in Melbourne

Typeset in 10.5/13.5pt ITC Giovanni LT

National Library of Australia Cataloguing-in-Publication Data

Author:	Mesiti, Pat.
Title:	The $1 million reason to change your mind / Pat Mesiti.
ISBN:	9781742168944 (pbk.)
Notes:	Includes index.
Subjects:	Wealth.
	Success.
	Finance, Personal.
	Motivation (Psychology).
Dewey Number:	330.16

Printed in Australia by McPherson's Printing Group

10 9 8 7 6 5 4 3 2 1

Author photos by Karla Majnaric

Cover designed by Brad Maxwell

Disclaimer
The material in this publication is of the nature of general comment only, and does not represent professional advice. It is not intended to provide specific guidance for particular circumstances and it should not be relied on as the basis for any decision to take action or not take action on any matter which it covers. Readers should obtain professional advice where appropriate, before making any such decision. To the maximum extent permitted by law, the author and publisher disclaim all responsibility and liability to any person, arising directly or indirectly from any person taking or not taking action based upon the information in this publication.

Contents

Foreword		*v*
About the author		*ix*
Introduction		*xi*
Chapter 1	Do you have a mind virus?	1
Chapter 2	Change direction to head for prosperity	13
Chapter 3	Your thoughts become your actions	31
Chapter 4	Developing a millionaire mindset	49
Chapter 5	Climbing the walls in your mind	57
Chapter 6	Developing a healthy view of yourself	71

Chapter 7   The 10 key characteristics of a
             millionaire mindset   79

Chapter 8   Fixing your attitude to money   87

Chapter 9   Make failure your teacher   97

Chapter 10   Know what you want   105

Chapter 11   Pay attention   119

Chapter 12   Growth happens by choice   135

Chapter 13   How to make good decisions   159

Chapter 14   Get some help!   167

Chapter 15   Aim for the stars   177

Chapter 16   Fuel your dream with passion   191

Chapter 17   Fuel your passion with a reason   201

Conclusion   *209*

Foreword

I'd argue that everybody's looking to get ahead in this world. It's the natural way — humans were built to want more! Luckily, we were also built to help others; to give them a hand-up. But none more than Pat Mesiti. This is why *The $1 Million Reason to Change Your Mind* is such an important book. Pat has used his infectious positivity and experience in gaining prosperity to share with you some secrets that will help you succeed.

We are not necessarily born with knowledge of how to increase our prosperity. We all deserve help to get us where we want to go — we just have to ask for it, learn from what we are told and then apply our new knowledge and watch our lives change for the better.

Contrary to the stereotype, prosperous people are not all sitting in their mansions, counting their cash. They are normal people who have simply discovered their goal, focused on it and gone after it. They are no different to you and me. They just attained a millionaire mindset, wherein they realised that we all need to rid ourselves of old thought processes that have held us back. Sure, they may have made some tough decisions or sacrifices to gain their goal, but their growth will surely have counterbalanced any kind of hardship they have undertaken.

One thing this book has taught me is the importance of mentors. The adage 'those who can, do; those who can't, teach' is rendered meaningless by Pat. He can do *and* he teaches. And, like any teacher worth his salt, he continues to learn. Pat may be seen as an expert in his field, but this is only because he is continually updating and renewing his knowledge. He claims always to have a book in his briefcase, and that if anyone catches him without one, they will be given a thousand dollars in cash. Next time you see Pat at a conference, see if you can catch him out! My bet is that it will be a fruitless exercise.

Never have I met a more positive man than Pat. He maintains his positivity even when he has to tell you you're stuffed. This is because he believes that any bad situation is not a full stop — it is an ellipsis. There's always somewhere to go, something to do to improve the situation. And if, in the depths of despair, you can't see the path, Pat will happily shine a light.

Those who have been lucky enough to see Pat speak know that I am right about this — he tells stories that you wouldn't believe if you didn't know him. Pat finds himself in situations where you or I might feel lost and uncomfortable, though there he sits, happy as a pig in mud. He could be hugging a bag lady or talking to a roomful of prisoners — or real estate agents! — but the message is always the same: find a dream and work towards it. With the right mindset, you will get there!

Another of Pat's points with which I passionately agree is the idea that in order to receive, you must give. Giving implies a millionaire mindset, which can only lead you onwards and upwards. Pat and his family are first-class philanthropists. They are responsible for feeding 6000 hungry mouths in the Third World. They have all they need and share the rest with people less fortunate than themselves. This is something more people in the world need to learn. We are all in this together, so why not help out a neighbour in need?

We all deserve a helping hand, so let Pat do what he is passionate about: helping others to become a more prosperous version of themselves — you, version 2.0! This is his passion and, as Pat says himself, 'Your passion is what will make your dream a reality.'

Read on and soak up what Pat Mesiti has to say — all he wants to do is share his prosperity and teach about the millionaire mindset. Then apply it to your life and watch it improve. Simple as that.

We're only given one life, so why not make the most of it?

Mark Victor Hansen
Co-creator, #1 New York Times best-selling series
Chicken Soup for the Soul ®
Co-author, *Cracking the Millionaire Code* **and**
The One Minute Millionaire
December 2008

About the author

Pat Mesiti is an author, speaker and prosperity activist with a passion to bring out the best in people. He is a highly effective income acceleration coach. His passion is to equip and empower people to experience growth and prosperity by helping them to reach their full potential.

Pat regularly speaks to sold-out audiences throughout the world and his books and materials have sold over two million copies. Pat's goal is to raise up ten thousand millionaires.

Introduction

I'm on a mission to help make people rich. And to do that, I mess with people's minds. That's why I've written this book. You may wonder what a book about mindsets has to do with you! Well, it's very simple: we all need to have the right kind of mindset to achieve wealth and prosperity. You see, prosperity isn't about money, it's about *mindsets*. Change your mindset and you can change your world.

You need to shift your thinking if your life is going to change. Let me ask you a question: if you want your life to prosper, will the same level of thinking that you currently have be good enough to get you to another level? The answer is no. The good news is that it is possible to change your thinking!

Does winning the lottery give you a million dollar mindset?

Do you think winning the lottery would solve all your problems? That you would spend the rest of your life flying to Paris to buy clothes, going to Italy to buy a new car, sitting by the pool at your 37-room mansion... Here's a story about a man who won the lottery — in fact, he won US$315 million!

At 55 years of age, Andrew Jackson 'Jack' Whittaker, Jr was living a successful, comfortable life in West Virginia, USA. By most standards, he had a well-rounded family life and a great job. On 25 December 2002, Whittaker stopped for some petrol. He also purchased some breakfast and a lottery ticket. That small piece of paper changed his life almost in an instant. He won the jackpot of US$315 million! His was the biggest ever lottery win in the United States at that time.

Right now you're probably thinking, *I wish that was me! I could do a lot with those millions!* But the tragedy of this story is that within four years, Whittaker lost it all! Today, Whittaker claims that he's struggling to pay his many debts. He says that no amount of money loaned to friends and family was ever enough and that his lottery win destroyed his life. In fact, he says that if he could do it all over again, he would have just filled up his tank, bought breakfast and gone on his merry way.

You must be a millionaire in your head first

How many times have you read stories about people who have won a fortune in the lottery and a few years later they are back on Poverty Street? In his recent book, *Win In Business*, Gloria Jean's Coffees co-founder, Peter Irvine, said:

> *For far too many people a sudden increase in wealth ruins their attitude, their relationships and their business. The reason is that they never learned how*

to earn the wealth and they never learned how to manage it.

World champion boxer Mike Tyson squandered earnings of more than $300 million — today he is bankrupt and has a long list of creditors to pay. How do you lose that much money? I'll tell you how: the same way many of us waste away $1000 — or even $10 000. It's not really about the money. It has a lot to do with your mindset and your attitude to money. You cannot move to another level of prosperity and success with your current mindset. That's why so many of us waste away large sums of money that suddenly end up in our hands. Our mindsets haven't risen to the level of our new wealth. That's why you need to change your mindset — so that you can go up another level of wealth and prosperity... and flourish there.

You cannot move to another level of prosperity and success with your current mindset.

When love came to town

A few years ago, I was in New York City and I'd been asked to speak as part of a street program run by one of the local communities. We had a few counsellors and a salsa band there and, as the program got underway, I wondered what I should speak about. The streets were dark and there were a few crack houses close by. There was evidence of violence everywhere, but no evidence of a visible audience.

When the time came, I stood up and spoke on the topic 'When love comes to town'. I spoke about the power of love and I shared my story. I talked about where I had come from and what I understood to be love: love is gentle, love is kind, love is patient, love doesn't rejoice in doing wrong, love doesn't hold grudges...

My friend Danny, who was running the program, said to me, 'Pat, we want to help these people, so invite them to come forward off the street if they want help and food.'

I turned and said to him, 'But Danny, there's nobody here!'

I've learned not to mess with Danny, so I invited people to come forward if they needed help or food. All of a sudden, people started coming out of the crack houses, pushing their trollies. It looked like a scene from Michael Jackson's *Thriller*!

As I was standing there, a guy came up to me and he smelled of booze and vomit. This man's hair was all matted together. As he came closer I could see lesions through his beard. They were all over his face — the result of HIV infection. He stunk unbelievably.

He whispered to me in a husky voice, 'Hey! You talk about love... Do you love me?'

I took two steps back, but said, 'Yeah, I love you.'

He said to me, 'If you love me, you hug me!'

A little voice inside me that I've come to know said to me, *Hug him!*

You *hug him!* I thought in reply, but I asked him his name and reached out. Hector stepped into my arms. I then realised that I couldn't smell him anymore, but I could feel his pain.

Through tears he began to tell me what had happened that morning. 'I was going through the trash this morning and I found an old cup of coffee,' he said. 'Something came over me and I prayed, "God, if you're there, get someone to hug me today." I've never been hugged.'

Well, we welcomed Hector into that community and, sure enough, love came to town! We cleaned him up and found him some work.

Two years later I went back to that community in New York and I asked my friend Danny where I could find Hector.

'Hector is dead, man!' he said.

I was devastated. I had been so looking forward to seeing Hector again. Danny saw the look on my face and whacked me. (Danny has no compassion!)

'Hey, Mr Motivation!' he said. 'What's your problem? You got a philosophical problem, man? Sometimes there is something far greater than just breathing air. Come with me!'

He took me to a back room of the community facility where he worked. In that room I saw about 150 people — old people, young people, black people and white people. Some of them had headsets on their heads and they were peering at television screens, computer screens and laptop screens... all these people were working!

'Hey, everybody look at me!' Danny shouted. Everyone turned around to look at Danny. 'You!' he pointed at one of them and said, 'Get up! Tell Pat your story!'

This man stood up and said, 'My name is Eduardo. I was a gang member, man. I would pop people for $20. Then Hector came into my life!'

Danny pointed to a woman. She stood up and said, 'My name is Cindy. I was a street worker. I used to waste my life. I was a junkie. Then Hector came into my life!'

Danny pointed to someone else, who also stood up. 'My name is Ricardo. I also used to do drugs, until Hector came into my life!'

Another man stood up. 'My name is Shaque. I used to pop guys. I used to deal drugs. Then Hector came into my life!'

One after the other, people stood up and told me how Hector came into their life. Danny turned to me and said, 'Sometimes the wealthiest man on the planet is the one who leaves a legacy for others.'

> The problem with a lot of us is that we have healthy bodies, but we've got viruses in our minds.

Hector had spent the last days of his life giving others what had been given to him: love and a second chance at building a better life.

I suddenly realised something. The only reason Hector was able to impact on all these lives was because nobody had told him he couldn't.

Healthy bodies, but viruses in our minds

Hector had a virus in his body, but he didn't have one in his mind. The problem with a lot of us is that we have healthy bodies, but we've got viruses in our minds. I'm going to help you change that!

At one level, Mike Tyson was an incredible achiever. He had a dream, he had goals and he pursued them with great determination and with great success. You might have a dream and hit every goal you set for yourself, but a dream in and of itself is not enough. Unless you are able to change your mindset to think how wealthy people think — to think with what I call a *millionaire mindset* — you won't achieve sustainable prosperity. Like lottery winners, you may gain a large sum of money next week, but without a millionaire mindset, it may soon disappear. The bottom line is that your income won't keep you where your mindset can't hold you.

You can change your thinking

If you learn to think differently, you will start to see better results in your personal and professional life.

A story is told of a Texan who walked into a church office one day and said to the secretary, 'I'd like to speak to the chief hog in the trough.'

'I beg your pardon!' she responded. 'Are you referring to our senior minister?'

'That's right,' he said.

She looked him in the eye and said, 'He's a man of integrity, he's a man of character, he's a man of the Scriptures and he's a man above reproach. How dare you speak about him in such a fashion!'

'Oh,' he said. 'I'm sorry. I have a cheque here for a million dollars that I wanted to give him for the church building fund.'

She immediately turned around and said, 'Hang on a minute. I think I see the big fat pig coming right now.' She had an instant change in mindset.

Motivational speaker Brian Willersdorf tells the story of a Baptist minister whose friend strode up to him one day and said, 'Look, my dog's sick. Could you pray for my dog?'

The minister responded, 'Buddy, we're Baptists. We pray for people, we don't do dogs, but I do know a good Catholic priest who could help you.'

The man looked at the minister and said, 'Well, what's his name?'

'His name is Father McKenzie,' said the minister.

'Well, would you please give Father McKenzie this cheque for $20 000 and thank him for praying for my dog?'

Quick as a flash the Baptist minister replied, 'Oh, you didn't tell me it was a Baptist dog!'

It's amazing how quickly we can change our mindsets when under pressure.

Learn to think for a change and you will see better results

How many times in your life have you dreamed about what it would be like to be wealthy? Many people spend their whole lives wishing they had more money, but never do anything about it. (Buying a weekly lottery ticket doesn't count!) The truth is, you can live a more prosperous life if you are prepared to make some changes.

The first place change needs to happen is in your mind.

The first place change needs to happen is in your mind. Before you can become a millionaire, you need to develop the *mindset* of a millionaire. This book is all about helping you to shift your thinking from a *poverty* mindset to a *millionaire* mindset. It isn't just about financial prosperity; it's also about mental and emotional wealth — it's about abundance and success in every area of your life. Prosperity definitely includes financial wealth, but it should never be limited to this. Prosperity is something that affects your whole life.

I will coach you on the journey through the pages of this book. People have coaches for a lot of reasons, but often we neglect some of the most important ones. Prosperity is an important part of life. My goal is to lead you into a new way of thinking, to help you to think logically — not just emotionally; to help you understand the difference between millionaire thinking and poverty thinking.

Decide that you're going to be a wealthy person

Generally speaking, genuine prosperity does not happen by accident. You *decide* to become prosperous. You have to be *committed* to prosperity. If you're not fully committed to becoming prosperous, then you can't blame anybody or anything else for your lack of it. Your upbringing, your job, your organisation, your education are not responsible for your prosperity. If you want to prosper, then there's only one person that matters — you! *You* have to decide that you are going to be a wealthy person.

As we work our way through this book, my aim is to help you begin to think differently. First, you have to think differently about yourself. You need to start seeing yourself as a person who *can* prosper. You may need to change some ingrained thinking patterns, or perhaps you'll need to overcome negative mindsets that have developed as a result of past experiences. You might also need to change how you think about wealth and money.

You have to change your thinking about your future. Your future is *not* predetermined. Rather, you create your future through the decisions and choices you make today. What you need is a dream — a clear vision of the future you want to create for yourself.

You may also need to change the way you think about other people. Instead of seeing others as competition or as obstacles you need to negotiate on your way to personal success, you need to see other people as a key to your own success. Other people need to become the ultimate purpose for our prosperity. What do I mean by this? Simply: our primary reason for pursuing prosperity has to be so that we can do something to make life better. Not just for ourselves, but for others as well.

Are you ready for a mind shift? Are you willing to get rid of wrong thought patterns that relate to yourself and your world and mindsets about money and wealth that have kept you contained? Are you willing to kick out those thought patterns, ideas and mindsets that have prevented you from stepping into the truly prosperous life that you were born to have and that is waiting to be uncovered?

Do you want to have a millionaire mindset?

Let's get started!

Challenges

Throughout this book, you'll find challenges to help you tackle the issues addressed. Take the time to complete these, as they will help you along the path to having a millionaire mindset.

Chapter 1

Do you have a mind virus?

I am tired of the mind viruses that are crippling people living in the western world — especially in my own nation. Sadly, Australia is becoming known as a nation of whingers. But it's not just evident in Australia — I see it in other countries as well. People want to change everything around them.

'If only I could live in a better suburb!' they say.

'If only my children could attend a better school!'

And, 'If only I could get a better paying job!'

Some of us want the economy to change. For some people there's too much rain. For others there's not enough rain. Some people don't like the summer and others don't like the winter. You can't change the economy, you can't change the weather and you can't change the seasons.

The answer to your problems is not out there, it's in your thinking; it's in your mindset.

Do you drink straight from the bottle?

A young man by the name of Bruce came to the drug rehabilitation centre I was running a few years ago. Bruce used to drink lime cordial straight from the bottle. (Cordial is a very sweet drink concentrate that must be diluted with water before consuming.) One day he saw someone mixing water with lime cordial. 'What are you doing?' he challenged. 'You're a real tightwad!'

Many [mind viruses] are caught during our childhood.

Surprised, the man turned to Bruce and said, 'Bruce, let me tell you something. You're not supposed to drink cordial straight from the bottle.'

Bruce drank lime cordial straight from the bottle because he didn't know any better. Many of us are like Bruce; we want a better life, we want to be prosperous, we want to improve our relationships, but we're going about it the wrong way and we just don't know any better!

What you don't know *will* hurt you. You must deal with the mentality that cripples and sabotages your finances, your relationships and your prosperity. The first thing you've got to do is shift your mindset, and the next thing you've got to do is get rid of some of your mind viruses.

Mind viruses

Before I show you how to create a millionaire mindset, you must first examine your current attitudes to money and your own financial situation. You can't change the way you think about money if you don't understand the mind viruses that might be infecting you.

Mind viruses are reflected as attitudes and thought patterns that have quietly and unobtrusively entered your mind over the years. Many of them are caught during our childhood. When we're young, we're vulnerable and we absorb both good and bad mindsets because we don't know any better.

Many of these viruses affect the way we think about money and success. If you catch these viruses, they limit your opportunities for success because they cause you to see everything as negative, as threats and as problems.

For example, for many of us, our reaction to bills shows we have a mind virus about bills. Don't focus on your bills; instead, focus on your assets. Me? I love receiving bills! You may think I have a problem, but it's true! Too many people shake in their boots when a bill arrives. If you're one of those people, you need to shift your mindset. Do you know what bills mean to me? They mean that I am *decreasing* my liabilities and I am *increasing* my assets! Now there's a real mindset shift!

Spotting the viruses

You can quickly recognise mind viruses in other people by the way they react to things, like the success of others. You can easily test whether someone has a mind virus by asking them questions. For instance, women could try this on their partner: next time you go shopping for a dress, ask your partner to go with you. When you see a really expensive dress, tell your husband or boyfriend, 'I've chosen this one! Isn't it nice!' Then watch for his reaction, because what comes out of his mouth will reveal whether he has a mind virus. If he says, 'Not that one! It's too expensive!' He has a mind virus.

You can also test whether your friends have mind viruses. Tell a friend about a CEO of a well-known corporation who recently resigned and was given a multimillion-dollar handout...and wait for your friend's response. Here's how they may respond: 'How could someone be paid so much money! Nobody's worth that much!'

If you're earning one million dollars and you're making the company one billion dollars, your earnings are small change! What your friend is really saying is, 'Why isn't that me?'

Would you want someone who is paid $50 000 to be controlling your country's investments? I don't think so! Highly paid heads of corporations are paid according to the value they bring to the company. A poverty mindset declares, 'Nobody's worth that much!' But a prosperous mindset says, 'Yes, but they increased the company's earnings this year a thousand-fold! They're worth it!'

Here are more ways to uncover mind viruses. Talk to a colleague about how wealthy people seem to have better tax avoidance strategies…Next time you are getting a haircut, talk about how so many celebrities end up divorced within a few short years…Talk to your colleagues about network marketing…Tell your parents you're giving up your job to pursue your dream of becoming a musician in a rock band…Take note of their reactions to see if you can spot any mind viruses.

Thirty examples of common mind viruses

Here are just 30 mind viruses I've spotted over the years — some of which you may have caught — and an example of a response from someone with a millionaire mindset:

Mind virus comment	Millionaire mindset retort
Money doesn't grow on trees!	That's obvious … money grows in your head.

Mind virus comment	Millionaire mindset retort
I'm not made of money!	No, you're made up of your thoughts.
We'd never be able to afford that!	Let's work out how we can afford it.
It's not whether you win or lose, it's whether you had fun that matters!	This is generally said by those who lose.
The rich get richer, the poor get poorer and the middle class go shopping!	A jealous and insecure person says this.
I didn't have it easy as a kid, so why should you?	If you are successful, then your kids have had to make sacrifices, so they should be rewarded.
Nobody ever gave me a free lunch!	Be the person who buys the lunch.
Money ruined my marriage!	No it didn't—you did it all by yourself!
Money made him greedy!	No it didn't—money magnified his greed!
You mustn't give people false hope!	People can't live without hope.
Do you think you are better than me?	Yes, I'm a work in progress.
The rich keep all the secrets to themselves!	Many successful, wealthy people run seminars and write books to help others become successful and wealthy.
Welcome to my humble home!	People say this out of a sense of false pride.

Mind virus comment	Millionaire mindset retort
I'm just an average Aussie battler!	There's nothing Aussie about being a battler!
Money is the root of all evil!	No it isn't—the love of money is the root of all evil!
Nobody in our family ever amounted to much!	The people who say this are the people who want to contain you.
Don't rock the boat!	People who say this don't want others to get ahead or achieve much.
I could never wear that! I could never drive that! I could never live there!	Try it—you might enjoy it.
Money won't make you happy!	Well, neither will being broke!
Life wasn't meant to be easy!	Don't try to make life easy—try to make life better!
Get an education so you can get a good job in a good company!	Working for someone else rarely makes people rich. Instead, become a business owner.
I wonder how many people he had to walk over to get to where he is!	In getting to where he is, I wonder how many people he helped.
That child has attention deficit disorder!	Not necessarily. If they're anything like me, they may just need to be taught some discipline or how to focus...We're too quick to medicate the magic out of children.

Mind virus comment	Millionaire mindset retort
I bet she's never done a hard day's work in her life!	We judge people according to our own intentions.
You've got to acknowledge your strengths, but focus on your weaknesses!	No, you'll only build prosperity out of your strengths.
That's impossible! It can't be done!	Impossible is a mindset, not a reality.
You don't have what it takes!	Learn to have what it takes.
It's been tried before. What makes you think you can succeed where others have failed?	Neil Armstrong was entitled to say, 'Many have tried to get to the moon and failed, but someone has to do it, so why can't I be the first?'
Some people are too ambitious!	If you shoot for the stars you may just hit the moon, but at least you've left the Earth.
We pay too much tax!	You don't earn enough.

Do you have any of these viruses? Chances are you do, and so do the people around you. But fear not! By the time you have finished reading this book, you will be free of them!

The results of mind viruses

Now, look at what happens when you let a mind virus affect your judgement. These people obviously had a virus, which meant they missed out on, or closed themselves off from, some pretty big opportunities:

There is no reason anyone would want a computer in their home!

—Kenneth Olsen, president, chairman and founder of Digital Equipment Corporation (1977).

Computers in the future may perhaps only weigh 1.5 tons.

—Popular Mechanics forecasting the development of computer technology (1949).

The horse is here to stay, but automobiles are only a passing novelty—a fad.

—The president of Michigan Savings Bank advising Horace H Rackham (Henry Ford's lawyer) not to invest in the Ford Motor Company in 1903. Rackham ignored him and bought stock, which he later sold for $12.5 million.

Man will never reach the moon, regardless of all the future scientific advances.

—Dr Lee De Forest, inventor of the vacuum tube and the father of radio (1967).

Television won't be able to hold onto any market it captures after the first six months. People will soon get tired of staring at a plywood box every night.

—Darryl F Zanuck, head of 20th Century Fox (1946).

I have no political ambitions for myself or my children.

—Joseph P Kennedy (1936).

What use could this company make of an electrical toy?

—Western Union president William Orton rejecting Alexander Graham Bell's offer to sell his struggling telephone company to Western Union for $100 000 (1876).

I confess that in 1901 I said to my brother Orville that man would not fly for 50 years. Ever since, I have distrusted myself and avoided all predictions.

—Wilbur Wright, US aviation pioneer (1908).

Who the hell wants to hear actors talk?

—Harry M Warner of Warner Brothers Studios (1927).

The Aussie battler mind virus

One of the mind viruses that has pervaded Australian culture is the myth of the 'Aussie battler'. I have to admit that this is one of my pet hates. The concept of the Aussie battler is nothing more than a negative mindset that keeps people suppressed and contained. It discourages entrepreneurship and it is a misnomer. It shows a hand-out mentality. People with this mindset say, 'People owe me. The government owes me. Big business owes me. My workplace owes me.' Here's some news: nobody owes you *anything*. Instead, you owe life. There is nothing proud about the 'I'm a battler; I'm owed' mentality.

When we look at any nation's history, everyone who struggled, even though they may have failed, was honoured for their valour and their conduct in hard times. The 'battler' mindset—which, by the way, exists in many cultures outside Australia—wants to tear down that which succeeds and expects to be rewarded for laziness, ignorance and non-achievement. People with this mindset want to be rewarded just for turning up. The reality is that nobody owes you.

There's nothing Australian about being a battler.

There's nothing Australian about being a battler. Australians are meant to be achievers, not battlers. There's nothing 'battler' about Rupert Murdoch, Ian Thorpe, Nicole Kidman, Steve Irwin, Kylie Minogue, Russell Crowe, Lleyton Hewitt, Greg Norman, Don Bradman, the Anzacs, the 800 horsemen who liberated Beersheba—or any other great Australians who made their mark on the world over the past two centuries. Australia is *not* a nation of battlers.

The 'Aussie battler' label creates a particular mindset that says that if you are a true Aussie, then you must be doing it tough and you're always going to be the underdog. This ridiculous notion is responsible for centuries of Australians who have lived far beneath their potential level of prosperity.

A few years ago, the Australian Government introduced a financial support system for families with children. They were giving all families—those they love to call 'average Aussie battlers'—a certain amount of money each month for family support. I immediately rang the government department that administered the payments and refused to accept the money. Why? Because I am not an Aussie battler and I refuse to allow that mindset any space in my life. I do not want to see myself as a battler. I am a winner, a victor, a high achiever and a walking prosperity machine.

Challenge:
Recognise your mind viruses and reject them

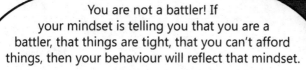

You are not a battler! If your mindset is telling you that you are a battler, that things are tight, that you can't afford things, then your behaviour will reflect that mindset.

You can never be prosperous if the mindset that governs your life and actions is one of disbelief and negativity. Recognise it as a mind virus and fight to reject it.

We aren't battlers, we are winners and we are achievers!

Chapter 2

Change direction to head for prosperity

If you are totally satisfied with the level of prosperity in your life right now, then you have no incentive to change. Perhaps you would like to be more wealthy, but have resigned yourself to the 'fact' that 'this is as good as it's going to get'. In other words, your level of discontent is not sufficient to motivate you to strive for change.

Before there can be any change in your life, you must acknowledge that things are not as good as they could or should be. Then you must resolve to do something about the level of prosperity in your life. Change starts with a decision to do something about a situation with which you are dissatisfied. In order to increase your prosperity, there needs to be some serious discontent in your life to spur on the decision to change. As soon as you become content with the level of prosperity in your life, you have set the limits of your prosperity.

Contentment means containment, and you were never meant to be contained. You were created with unlimited capacity, but your capacity to increase your prosperity depends on your level of discontent. This doesn't mean that you should live life in a constant state of frustration, dissatisfaction and disappointment, never being able to enjoy or appreciate what you have. No, like the athlete who is always pursuing his or her next 'personal best', there should always be a desire in us to grow, to increase and to go one level better. As the famous banker David Rockefeller once observed, 'If necessity is the mother of invention, discontent is the father of progress.'

I was recently given the privilege of speaking to a consulting company that helps build medium-to-large businesses. It was such an outstanding event that at the end of the sessions, so many people lined up at my resource table to purchase my books and other teaching materials that I felt like Speedy Gonzales trying to cope with the rush! About an hour later, as I was packing up my resources, a lady walked into the room, stormed right up to me, and said, 'Are you still open for business?'

The convener of the event stood beside me and shook his head. However, I looked at her with a smile and said, 'We're always open for business! How can I help you?'

She said to me, 'I want to buy your entire package of resources. I just went home and all my husband did for the entire time I was home was nag and complain about the bills and the creditors. He even said he wished we had never got into business. I thought to myself, *I've got a choice here: either my husband's going to mess with my head or Pat Mesiti is!* So I've come back to buy all your material. If I have a choice between listening to your advice and my husband's advice, I'll choose you every time!'

That's what I love doing. I want to mess with your head so that we can unscramble the eggs of your life and increase your prosperity.

Unfortunately, many of us fail to pursue prosperity because we may just be too comfortable. Think about your life for a moment. How satisfied are you with the level of prosperity in your life right now? Do you have a strong desire to be more prosperous? Or are you content with where you're at?

Middle-class comfort anaesthetises us to the possibilities of a prosperous future. Because of comfort, we settle for far less than what we are destined to become.

> Because of comfort, we settle for far less than what we are destined to become.

Any champion will tell you that you must experience pain and discomfort along the journey towards achievement, prosperity and abundance. The great football coach Vince Lombardi once said, 'The price of success is hard work, dedication to the job at hand, and the determination that whether we win or lose, we have applied the best of ourselves to the task at hand.' Unfortunately for many, our comforts anaesthetise us from getting started. I'm going to help you break out of this cycle and change direction, so that you are heading for prosperity rather than mediocrity.

Change direction!

A little while ago I spoke at a financial planning seminar. A prominent Australian sportsman came up to me after I had spoken and said, 'I really enjoyed what you said. You really fired me up. Mr Mesiti, I heard you helped a lot of my friends and I want you to help me. I am so motivated, I'll go the extra mile!'

In my mind I thought, *Son, let's just get through the first one!* Here's the problem with motivation: most people think motivation changes you. Motivation doesn't change you, knowledge does!

Jim Rohn once said, 'The fallacy of motivation is this: if you're driving down the road in the wrong direction, you don't need me to motivate you to drive faster. You need someone to say, "Stop! Change direction!"'

This young sportsman had great motivation, but media reports were saying he was out of control. He had just signed a multimillion-dollar deal. He had a full pocket, but an empty head. I want people to have a full head, a full heart *and* a full pocket!

> I want people to have a full head, a full heart *and* a full pocket!

You may have met people with a full head and empty pockets. They know it all, but they are broke. You may also have met people who have a full heart — they're waiting for the universe to bring everything to them. They don't want to work, they don't want to plan, they don't want to invest, and they don't want to give. These people are full of good intentions, but there's nothing in their heads and they are always broke. Other people have full pockets, but they have empty heads and empty hearts. They have nothing filling their mind or their inner world. This was the case with my friend — he had a full pocket, but an empty head.

He looked at me again and said, 'I want to be a great rugby league player! Can you help me?'

I looked at him and said, 'Don't you mean that you want to be a great person?'

He said, 'Yeah, that's right. I just want to be a great player. I want to be recognised as one of the legends of the game!'

I asked him how he would rate himself on a scale from one to 10 as both a player and as a person. I look at the whole person and I wanted him to do the same — you can't compartmentalise your life.

'I believe I'm an eight out of 10,' he replied.

'Come on — I've seen you play!' I said.

'But I've played for Australia!'

'Yes, you did,' I said. 'And you lost to New Zealand 34 to nil because you went on a drunken rampage throughout the city the night before the game.'

He hung his head and said, 'Okay, I'm a six out of 10.'

I knew he was a great player. I knew he had represented Australia. And I knew he wanted to go to another level, like most of us. If I asked you the question, *Do you want to go to another level?* You would answer yes! If I asked you, *Do you want to go to another level of investments?* You would answer yes! If I asked you the question, *Do you want to go to another level of income?* You would answer yes!

So I proceeded to run through a few qualifications with him. I said to him, 'Number one, I want you to train 30 minutes longer than everybody else on the team.'

'I can do that!' he said.

I said, 'Number two, I want you to stop going out late at night and getting boozed up six nights a week.'

He looked at me, hesitated, and then said, 'Okay, I can do that.'

I then said, 'Number three, I want you to change your friends.' Now, I'm not a killjoy, but I wanted to get this point across: your associations in life equal your assimilations. If your child came home today and introduced you to his or her new friend who had a swastika tattooed on his head, most of his teeth missing and holding an Uzi submachine gun, you would be slightly concerned! Here's why: you know your child can be influenced by that person.

I said to this young sportsman, 'I want you to change your

friends, because every relationship in your life will either feed a strength or a weakness in you. If you want to grow to another level, you've got to hang around people who will feed your strengths, not your weaknesses.'

'Number four, do you have a car?' I asked.

When he replied that he did, I asked, 'What's the most important part of the car?'

He said, 'The engine.'

I said, 'No, it's the CD player.'

'Why is that important?' he asked.

'Son, you have got to fill your head if you want to be great. Knowledge changes you. Here's some great motivational material I want you to listen to.' I gave him teaching material from some of the world's greatest speakers. 'I want you to use your sound system for something that will fill your mind, fill your heart and fill your pocket...and add value to your friends, your colleagues and your team.'

My last qualification was the clincher for this young man. I said, 'Finally, I want you to stick to one girlfriend.'

He looked at me and said, 'I can't do that! I'm a sports star!'

'Then stay average,' I said, 'because you're never going to be great!'

Here is the problem: this guy wanted to go to another level — he wanted to go from a six-out-of-10 person to an eight-out-of-10 person — but he didn't want to change.

Most of us think that everything outside of us needs to change. You may say to me, 'But Pat, if I didn't have to pay taxes I would be more prosperous.' Not true. Others may say, 'Pat, if fuel prices were lower I would be more prosperous.'

Not true. If everything changes in your life — your car, your house, your suburb, your employment and your income — but you didn't change, nothing would change. One of the first laws that govern prosperity is that you must be committed to the change you desire.

Discontent takes us beyond desire to a place where action becomes not simply an option, but an imperative. If prosperity is only an option to you, you will never achieve it.

To get started on the path to increased prosperity, prosperity needs to become not merely an option, but a lifestyle that you are totally committed to achieving. It is a lifestyle that affects every area of your world — your thinking, your relationships, your health and, of course, your finances. It's a lifestyle that transforms not just your outer world, but also who you are as a person. Desire alone is not enough. It takes discontent and focus to advance. It requires a willingness to make some sacrifices, to change the way you think and live. It takes a serious commitment to address areas of your life that are not working for you, even if it means you have to leave your comfort zone. You will never become the person you want to be by remaining just as you are.

> If prosperity is only an option to you, you will never achieve it.

You will never change what you consistently tolerate

Are you sick of remaining stuck at your current level of prosperity? Are you frustrated with the areas that are lacking in your life? Do you tolerate a small-thinking mindset? What happens is this: we tolerate and then we navigate. What do I mean by this? When we tolerate the things that hold us back, we find ourselves constantly having to navigate around them by making excuses for being the way we are. But if you don't tolerate, then you will no longer navigate. Instead, you will *instigate*. You will instigate new habits, new behaviours and new ways of thinking in your life. Remember, you will never change what you consistently tolerate.

Some people are always complaining about their lives. They say, 'I hate being broke!', 'My staff are always late!', 'I hate being unhealthy!', 'I don't like my bad temper!' and 'I don't like my bad spending habits!' How often do you catch statements like that leaving your mouth? As much as you might say you hate certain things in your life, the truth is you don't really hate them *enough*. If you really hated these things, you wouldn't tolerate them.

> Remember, we will never change what we consistently tolerate.

For example, I don't like beetroot. In fact, I hate it with a passion. The worst kind of punishment for me would be eating nothing but beetroot for the rest of my life. So, because I don't like it, I don't eat it. Because I don't like it, I don't tolerate it. I don't tolerate it in a hamburger. I don't tolerate it in a salad. I simply refuse to have beetroot in my life. Therefore, if a smoker says to me, 'I hate smoking!' my reply is, 'Then why do you smoke? If you really hated it, you wouldn't tolerate it — you wouldn't smoke!' When we really hate something, we refuse to tolerate it.

Your level of discontent will give in to change

Prosperity is hindered by what you won't give up. Here is another illustration. A friend of mine was living in a run-down part of town. It was a government housing area where all the houses were painted canary yellow. One day a man turned up at his house and gave it a fresh coat of canary yellow paint.

My friend hated the colour of his house. He didn't like living in that area, but he had tolerated it for many years. On the day that man came and painted his house canary yellow, he finally decided he'd had enough. His level of discontent finally reached a point where putting up with the status quo was no longer an acceptable option. He decided he would not allow himself to continue to be contained by his upbringing. He said to his wife, 'We will never have our house painted canary yellow again!'

Then he began to make some changes. He decided to take hold of a small business opportunity and stopped spending lazy days in front of the television flicking from channel to channel. He began to work hard at his new, small home-based business. He worked hard and, today, my friend lives in a 10-bedroom house with a pool. He has a view of the water in one of the most prestigious beachfront areas in Australia. Realising he had a choice, he stopped tolerating unsatisfactory circumstances and he began to instigate change. As a result, he no longer lives in a canary yellow house.

You will never change what you are constantly prepared to tolerate. One of my favourite quotes is, 'Change is not change until something changes.' The longer you tolerate inconsistency, a sense of lacking, laziness, inactivity and bad habits in your life, the longer you are delaying your prosperity. Constant change is a permanent condition in the life of any successful person. Warren Bennis of the Leadership Institute said this: 'In life, change is inevitable; in business, it is vital.'

Stephen Covey, author of *The 7 Habits of Highly Effective People*, said, 'If you keep doing what you're doing, you'll keep getting what you're getting!' I would add to his statement, 'So if you don't like what you're getting, don't tolerate it ... change it!'

Break your habits or they will break you

The first step towards becoming more prosperous is to make a decision and declare, 'I am not staying here any longer!' My friend in the canary yellow house hit a crisis point. If the desire for something greater doesn't drive you to change, then a crisis generally will. Robert H Waterman, co-author of *In Search of Excellence*, says, 'Habit breaking is a prerequisite for change and renewal. It needs more than a simple decision. It takes motivation, desire and will.'

The millionaire mindset is all about prosperity. The word 'prosperity' means 'to bloom, to flourish, to progress, to succeed and to thrive'. It is all about continual advancement in every area of your life. If you ever think you have finally arrived at where you want to be in life, then you have reached the end of the road to prosperity. Prosperity must be seen as a journey, not a destination. The fact is that you never actually arrive at prosperity. It involves the continual evolution of your mind, your will, your emotions, your relationships, your wealth and every other area of your life.

> [Prosperity] is all about continual advancement in every area of your life.

In 1870, a man called Russell H Conwell was riding a camel caravan along the valley between the Tigris and Euphrates Rivers in Mesopotamia when one of the guides began to entertain a group of tourists with some local tales. The then 27-year-old Conwell was deeply impressed by the story of a rich Persian farmer named Ali Hafed.

One day Ali heard a Buddhist priest speaking about mythical diamond fields in some faraway land. Ali decided to give up his own fruitful lands to go and search for this immense wealth. For many years Ali Hafed travelled far and wide. He grew old and poor and eventually died far from home, a disillusioned and broke old man.

Tragically, soon after his death, acres of fabulous diamonds were found on Ali Hafed's own land. The story of Ali Hafed had a huge impact on Conwell and he formed a truth that he would live by for the rest of his life: 'Your diamonds are not in faraway mountains or in distant seas; they are in your own backyard if you will but dig for them.'

The exciting truth in all this is that the starting point of the quest for a millionaire mindset is wherever you are *right now*. No matter who you are, or what you know or don't know about money and wealth, or what your current circumstances are, or what has happened to you in the past, if you simply make a firm decision today to do something to change your world, then you are at the starting point of seeing increased prosperity in your life.

Challenge:
Start changing

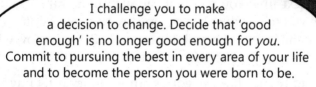

I challenge you to make a decision to change. Decide that 'good enough' is no longer good enough for *you*. Commit to pursuing the best in every area of your life and to become the person you were born to be.

You're now at the starting line of your journey to develop a millionaire mindset.

Change direction to head for prosperity

You can't have a broke head and a full pocket

On a recent flight to the United States with my colleague, Greg, I found myself having an interesting conversation with two men sitting in front of us. At some point, one of them asked me why I was going to the US.

'I'm on a speaking tour,' I answered.

'What do you speak about?' he asked.

'I speak about prosperity and abundance.'

He thought about that for a second, and then he stated, 'Money is not that important to me.'

I had just finished reading the brilliant book by T Harv Eker, *Secrets of The Millionaire Mind*. I quickly shot back a line from that book: 'You're broke, aren't you!'

The guy replied, 'Man, I've got peace. Money can't buy you peace.'

Let me ask you this question: would you be more at peace if you had a million dollars in the bank and a $10 million investment portfolio? Lack of money is actually one of the reasons so many people do not have peace.

'The next time you get your mobile phone bill,' I said, 'I want you to call the phone company and say, "I don't have much money, but I have lots of peace!" Do you know what they'll say to you? They'll tell you to *peace off*!'

He said to me, 'But I've got health — money can't buy you health!'

'No,' I said to him, 'but it can pay for medical expenses. If you're sick, money is a good thing to have.'

Then he said, 'But I have love — money can't buy you love!'

I said, 'Let me tell you something. Even if you were as ugly as a dog and you had lots of money, some women would still find you cute!'

This young man didn't have a millionaire mindset. He thought money was an evil thing. In actual fact, money can be an incredible tool, but it does make an awful master. The power of money lies in the mindset of the person who has it. This young man needed a mindset shift.

Every 60 seconds someone somewhere becomes a millionaire, according to Mark Victor Hansen and Robert Allen, authors of *The One Minute Millionaire*. Why can't that someone be you? Sometimes it takes a lifetime to make a million dollars — for others, it takes just a few years. But no matter how long the first million might be in coming, it always starts with a change of mindset. You need to ensure that your inner world and your outer world are in sync. Most people want to change their *outer* world, but they fail to address the need to change their *inner* world.

> You need to ensure that your inner world and your outer world are in sync.

All of us have internal blockages to prosperity that we need to deal with before we can see significant external change. There is a verse in the Bible that says, 'I pray that you may prosper in all things and be in health, just as your soul prospers.'

The Greek word for 'soul' is *psuche*, from which we get the word 'psyche', which refers to the mind. This verse succinctly expresses the idea that there is a link between the prosperity of your mind and your prosperity in 'all things'.

Change begins in the mind

Your mind is like a filter through which you interpret the world and your own experiences; it is where you form your beliefs, attitudes and understanding of the nature of your 'reality'. No two people see a single situation the same way. The classic illustration of this is the difference between someone who sees a glass of water as half empty and the one who sees the same glass as half full — same glass, different perspectives. Why the difference? The minds of the two observers are filtering the information they receive about the glass differently. We would label the first person as a pessimist and the second as an optimist — you must be an optimist to prosper and fulfill your dreams.

Wealth [is] more about investing in something than it is about spending.

More important than categorising the different points of view is the need to understand why these two people see things the way they do. To begin with, one person is putting water into the glass while the other is taking it out. A millionaire mindset interprets wealth as more about investing in something than it is about spending. To continue with the water metaphor, do you see wealth in your life as a reservoir that is gradually running dry, or do you see it as an endless spring that is continually brimming over?

To begin the process of changing your mindset, you first need to understand how your mind's filter works and why it filters things the way it does. This will lead you to an understanding of why you need to change the way you think and the way you view the world. I'm not saying that we all need to get into some kind of in-depth psychotherapeutic experience. It's simply a matter of developing a basic understanding of why we think the way we do.

What shapes your views?

What shapes, or has shaped, your thinking and your world view? For example, how do you view money? Did you grow up in a home where all you ever heard from your parents were expressions like, 'We're not made of money', or, 'Money doesn't grow on trees'? Or perhaps your view of money is even more severe; maybe you grew up hearing statements such as 'Money is the root of all evil!' or 'Money ruined my marriage!' If your mindset is such that money is always incredibly hard to come by, or that money is inherently evil, you will need to change your philosophy about money before you can truly prosper.

What's your mindset? Have you bought into the mindset that is reflected in expressions such as 'The rich get richer, the poor get poorer and the middle class go shopping'? If you tell me your financial history, I will be able to describe your current mindset regarding money. I once had a client who was a successful businessman, but his goal was simply to break even. In fact, my nickname for him was 'Mr Break-even'. He inherited a break-even mindset from his father.

A millionaire mindset is not about breaking even; it's about breaking into abundance and profit.

How you think is how you act

Our outward behaviour will always conform to our internal mindset. That means if we want to change how we act, we first have to change how we think. Dr Maxwell Maltz, author of the classic self-help book *Psycho-Cybernetics*, has said, 'Ideas and actions that are contrary to a person's belief system will not be acted and will not be accepted.' What this means is that even if you think you want to be wealthy, but your life is currently governed by thoughts that you are lacking, then you will never achieve wealth.

It's all about how you think. You cannot have two opposing thoughts in one head. For example, you can't think happy and feel sad at the same time.

In order to bring about change in your external world, you have to work on your mind, your attitudes and the way you think about and construct your life.

In your day-to-day life, are you playing offence or defence? Are you waiting for your lucky break or are you busy creating your future? Are you focused on end results or on the process? Are you blaming your past or confronting it? You cannot change what you won't confront. Wrong mindsets that are not confronted will take a strong hold over your mind. We become so used to them that we begin to think of them as a natural part of who we are. We say, 'That's just the way I think. It's who I am. I can't change who I am.' Yes, you can! You need to change what you constantly tolerate. You need to confront thought patterns and mindsets that keep your prosperity locked up and you need to be determined to change them.

> ... Developing a millionaire mindset sets you up for great achievement.

The wise man is the master of his mind

An ancient proverb says that the wise man is the master of his mind, but the fool will be its slave. You need to be the master of your own mind. One of my favourite expressions is this: 'If it's a mist in your mind, then it's a fog around your world.' In other words, if you are not clear in your mind, then your whole world will appear as if through a fog.

Your mind needs to be like a thermostat, rather than a thermometer. A thermometer reacts to the external environment, but a thermostat is proactive and is able to change its environment. To change the climate of a room or a building, you set the thermostat.

Your thoughts are the roots of your life. In order to change the fruit of your life, you first need to change the roots. Be aware of *why* you think the way you think. Thought patterns can be deep-rooted, so make a decision to become more aware of them and their origins. There are some thought patterns in your life that you need to uproot if you are to ever become prosperous.

Statistician W Edwards Deming, initiator of *Total Quality Management*, found from 50 years of statistical study that if you focus on the first 15 per cent of any process and get it right, you will go on to achieve at least 85 per cent of your desired outcome. That's why having the right mindset is so important; developing a millionaire mindset sets you up for great achievement.

Challenge:
Decide to rise above average

Before we go any further, think about your mindset right now. What influences in your life—past and present—have shaped the way you think about wealth and prosperity? Are you a 'glass half full' or a 'glass half empty' kind of person? What are your expectations? Is your goal in life just to get by or to break even? If so, why do you think that way? What thought patterns and mindsets have you been tolerating instead of confronting? Are you ready to confront wrong thinking or will you just 'stay average'?

Chapter 3

Your thoughts become your actions

Your mindset sets the course of your life. A mindset is a frame of mind or a pattern of thinking. The millionaire mindset is no different — it's a way of thinking about your potential for wealth and prosperity that creates positive expectation and motivates you to action. Mindsets are formed in the process of interpreting our experiences — things that are said to us, things that are done to us, the way we see people treating each other. If we develop wrong mindsets on the basis of negative experiences, we end up living at a level far beneath where we could and should be living. A wrong mindset can set us on a course towards disaster. People can often avoid calamity in their lives simply by changing their thinking.

Have you ever looked at a person's clothes and thought, *What were they thinking when they dressed this morning?* Remember the bell-bottoms and flares of the '70s? Mine were so wide it took two days for the back to catch up to the front! What were we thinking? The answer is that we didn't really think about it; we wore what we were told was the fashion of the day. When you see the predicaments that people can get themselves into, it often makes you wonder what they were thinking.

Garbage in, garbage out

Most wrong thinking is based on wrong information or a wrong premise. If you start with a wrong premise, you will come to a wrong conclusion for all the wrong reasons. For example, if my premise is 'people look cool in bell-bottoms', then my conclusion will be that if I put on a pair of bell-bottoms I will look cool. Wrong!

> Most wrong thinking is based on wrong information or a wrong premise.

I remember once speaking at a conference in New Zealand to a group of young people. There was a young guy standing at the back of the room who I thought looked really mean. I interpreted his folded arms and tattooed face as an indication that he was a troublesome person and I became wary of him as I spoke.

Imagine my surprise when I discovered that he was a Sunday school teacher! I had started with a wrong premise; that anyone who looked like him must be bad news. I formed a wrong conclusion for all the wrong reasons. That's what prejudice is — prejudging a person or situation before we have all the facts.

I have also been on the receiving end of this kind of prejudice. A very successful friend of mine once gave me a solid gold watch as a gift. It was a beautiful watch. It had a diamond face and bezel and was worth about $40 000. At the time, I was involved in running life development programs and events for young people around Australia and abroad. I was also running rehabilitation programs for young people with life-controlling addictions and was working with the poor and underprivileged. I had been quite successful in my work and I was often invited to speak at youth conventions and other such events. I'd also written a number of books that had sold well.

By the same token, I was not at the point in my life where I could buy myself a $40 000 watch!

One day I was signing books at a conference when a gentleman noticed my watch. He came up to me with a look of disgust and contempt. He proceeded to tell me that I was a charlatan and a thief. He couldn't fathom that a person who was working among the poor and helping young people with drug addictions and other problems could afford a watch like that. At first I didn't respond. I watched him as he proceeded to tell everybody around us what a charlatan he thought I was.

Later that day, when I stepped up onto the platform to speak, I told the story of how my friend had given me my watch. The first person at the book table afterwards was my accuser. He told me how sorry he was that he had misjudged me. Without knowing the circumstances of how I had come to own such a nice watch, this man had formulated a wrong premise — that is, that someone who did what I did could only come to own such a watch by dishonest means — and this had led him to a wrong conclusion about me.

After he had apologised to me, I took a piece of paper, tore it into little pieces and threw them into a fan. I said to the man, 'I want you to put that piece of paper back together just as it was.'

'I can't do that!' he exclaimed.

'Exactly,' I replied. 'It can't be done. But that's just what you have done to my name and my credibility. You have formulated a wrong premise and you came to a wrong conclusion about me for all the wrong reasons.'

We are often too quick to arrive at wrong conclusions based on a wrong premise. If you want to be a great thinker, if you want to be a person with a great capacity for wealth and prosperity, if you want to develop a millionaire mindset, then you have got to base your thinking on the right premise. The thinking that has brought you to where you are now will not take you to where you want to be.

Thoughts become things

Bad thoughts can never produce good results and good thoughts won't produce bad results. Always remember the saying: thoughts become things. Achieving a millionaire mindset requires a higher level of thinking. Our thoughts determine our lives. The input of our thoughts determines the output of our actions.

Here's how it works: it starts with *awareness*. You need to become aware of *how* you think and *why* you think the way you do.

Once you've developed this awareness of your thinking, you are in a position to change how you *think*. If you change your thinking, it will change how you *feel*. If you change your feelings, it will change how you *act*. If you change your actions, it will change your level of prosperity — and how you *live*. It's a five-stage process:

Awareness → Think → Feel → Act → Live

If you become aware of how and why you think a certain way, you can end up changing the way you live, whether it's in the area of your finances, your relationships, your possessions or your business. Please note that this does not work in reverse. You must understand that some people want to change the way they live without changing the way they think. It simply doesn't work that way.

Isn't it amazing that most people who have made great fortunes have also lost them? They tend to bounce back stronger, quicker and better. Why? Because they already had the right mindset and they learned from their mistakes. It was that positive, right thinking that gave them the valuable experience to know how to rebuild their fortunes. Some of the people who are billionaires today have lost great amounts of money, and they have all bounced back stronger—not the same, or weaker, but stronger. You see, it depends on your level of thinking. When you ask them for tips on how to build your fortune, they don't say, 'Well, invest in this stock and buy these shares.' No, they say, 'Think big! Have a great attitude. Develop good people skills.' They always focus on what is inside you, rather than on external forces.

> The thinking that has brought you to where you are now will not take you to where you want to be.

Feelings, nothing more than feelings ... You think so?

Sometimes people want to start changing at the level of feelings, but the key to changing our feelings is to first change our thinking. Here's a practical illustration of how this works: have you ever been in love? And have you ever felt annoyed with the person you love?

Our tendency is to accept our feelings as something we have no control over. 'I can't help my feelings,' you may say. Yes you can! You can choose to change your feelings by changing the way you think. Try to think positive thoughts about someone while continuing to feel angry about them. It's impossible! What we tend to do is to feed our feelings of anger by thinking negative thoughts about the person or situation with which we are angry. But if you make a choice to change the way you *think*, this will change the way you *feel* about the person, and that in turn will change the way you *act* towards them. Ultimately, this will change the way you *live*.

Before we move on, let's consider the topic of 'feelings' a little more. One of the biggest traps that you can fall into is the 'feeling' trap — allowing feelings to dictate the circumstances of your life. You need to bring them under the control of correct thinking. Your feelings should be a product of a millionaire mindset that is expressed through your words. They should be a support mechanism to your wealth creation capacity, not a destructive habit that robs you of prosperity.

...Confusion is nothing more than the inability to make a decision.

Feelings are fickle and they can deceive you. Most people *feel*, rather than *think* their way through life. If you want to change the way you feel, don't focus on your feelings, focus on your thinking. You can't think happy and feel sad at the same time. It's impossible. So focus on the primary cause of your negative feelings. Most of the issues we face in life are the result of the thinking that kickstarts your feelings.

Deal with the thinking first

So often we hear people say, 'I feel confused. I don't know what to do!' Now stop right there and consider this: confusion is nothing more than the inability to make a decision. Once you have made a decision, the confusion is gone. So deal with the thinking first.

Sometimes it seems that the whole world revolves around feelings; so much so that we become virtually enslaved by them. Feelings can be the biggest hindrance to change in our lives. One of the most common excuses for inaction is

'I didn't *feel* like doing it'. So many people live unfulfilled lives because all their action is driven purely by how they feel from one minute to the next. This works in other ways as well. The whole 'if it feels good, do it' philosophy is really just another way of saying, 'I'm a slave to my feelings.' Being driven by negative feelings will never lead us into positive action. We need to make our feelings subject to our thinking so that our actions are ultimately driven not by feelings, but by thought. Once again, if you can change your *thinking*, you will change your *feelings*, which in turn will change your *actions*, therefore, your *life*.

Feelings or thinking patterns?

Because of the link between our thoughts and our feelings, we sometimes confuse thinking patterns with feelings. Here are five thinking patterns that people often mistake for feelings:

1. *Enthusiasm.* Enthusiasm is a way of thinking that is all about how you approach things. Someone once said that an enthusiast is someone who is perfectly sure of the things about which he is mistaken. Henry Ford, founder of the Ford Motor Company, once said, 'Enthusiasm is at the bottom of all progress. With it there is accomplishment. Without it there are only alibis.'

   We need an enthusiastic mindset so that we always approach situations and opportunities with positive expectation. An enthusiastic mindset will translate into feelings of optimism.

2. *Attitude.* Attitude is a way of thinking that is all about how we view things. In the story of David and Goliath, the Israelite army had a perception that Goliath was too big to hit. David's perception of

the situation was that Goliath was too big to miss! Attitude is all about your mindset. Having a positive attitude puts us in a position to recognise and maximise every opportunity. As the American financier and presidential advisor Bernard Baruch said, 'You can overcome anything if you don't belly ache.' Winston Churchill once said, 'A pessimist sees a difficulty in every opportunity; an optimist sees the opportunity in every difficulty.'

3. *Happiness.* Many people think happiness is a feeling, but it is quite possible to be happy without necessarily *feeling* happy. Happiness is actually all about contentment and contentment is a mindset, not a feeling. You cannot be discontented *and* be happy. Abraham Lincoln said this: 'Most folks are as happy as they make up their minds to be.' Or as Martha Washington, wife of George, observed, 'I have learnt from experience that the greater part of our happiness or misery depends upon our dispositions and not upon our circumstances.'

4. *Depression.* Depression is a state of mind, not an emotional state. At one time in my life, I suffered from depression for over 18 months. Then one day I had what could almost be described as an awakening; I started to think, 'I don't want to be depressed anymore!' As a result of this change of mindset, I managed to throw off my depression. Depression results from a thought pattern that is all about hopelessness and gloom. To get rid of depression, you need to change the way you think.

I recently read a disturbing newspaper article about the increasing incidence of attention deficit hyperactivity disorder (ADHD) among children in countries such as Australia, Canada and the USA. The article reported that powerful cocktails of psychotropic drugs such as Ritalin are being prescribed for children as young as four years old, and in some cases the prescriptions are in adult doses. Some children are being given a range of medications for a range of apparent disorders in addition to ADHD, such as anxiety and depression. Needless to say, controversy is raging around this practice. Teachers have said that children on large doses of medication sit in class in a zombie-like state.

Attitude is all about your mindset.

Instead of medicating the magic out of our kids because we don't like the way they behave, we'd do better by trying to understand the underlying causes of their behavioural problems. You can't medicate thoughts that come from a broken heart; in situations like that you need to deal with the root causes before the resultant behaviour will change.

5. *Confidence.* When sportspeople are interviewed prior to participating in high-level competition, we often hear interviewers ask questions like, 'How confident are you feeling?' The truth is, confidence is a mindset, not a feeling. Confidence is a way of thinking based on your level of preparation. When you are well prepared, you are confident. You might feel nervous, but you are confident in the knowledge that you have prepared for the challenge you are about to face.

I have said that our actions are ultimately determined by our thoughts or mindsets. At the same time, however, behaviour can also influence our thought life. One of the behaviours that can often undermine our thought patterns is our speech. Usually, our words express our thoughts. But the words we speak can also have a significant influence on our mindsets. We need to pay close attention to the things we say and the words we allow to dominate important areas of our lives, such as our relationships, our financial world and our physical wellbeing.

Death and life are in the power of the tongue

Do you have little voices that talk to you? Sometimes those little voices scream loudly. And those inner voices sometimes become words in our mouth. Some people call it affirmation. Consider the following quotation from the Bible:

> We all make many mistakes, but those who control their tongues can also control themselves in every other way. We can make a large horse turn around and go wherever we want by means of a small bit in its mouth. And a tiny rudder makes a huge ship turn wherever the pilot wants it to go, even though the winds are strong. So also, the tongue is a small thing, but what enormous damage it can do. A tiny spark can set a great forest on fire. And the tongue is a flame of fire. It … can ruin your whole life. It can turn the entire course of your life into a blazing flame of destruction …

Words can be incredibly destructive. Wars have been started over nothing more than a few words. Words can destroy marriages and friendships. Words can also destroy human potential. Think about a time in your life where you felt devastated by someone else's words; the time as a small child you ran crying to your parents because one of your buddies told you that you weren't his friend anymore; the time the teacher told you you'd never amount to anything; the time someone criticised your work or told you that you weren't very good at something that you loved doing.

Consider what impact those words have had on your life.

On the other hand, words also have the capacity to create. Think of some of the great speeches of history: Abraham Lincoln's Gettysburg Address, Martin Luther King Jr's *I have a dream*, Winston Churchill's *We shall never surrender*.

Winston Churchill sent the English language to war along with his troops. He used the power of words to move and motivate his nation and the nations of the Allied forces.

Words have inspired whole nations and changed the course of history. People will pay hundreds of dollars to listen to great motivational speakers or to read their writings because of the great impact of their words on peoples' lives. (Hopefully you're having that kind of experience right now!) Think about a time in which you felt like you were on top of the world simply because someone said to you something as simple as, 'Well done!' Think about a time when someone else's words have inspired you to achieve something that you wouldn't otherwise have attempted. Think about the influence words have had on your life.

Think about the influence words have had on your life.

The good news is that if you know how to speak, then all the power of words is at your disposal. It's right there on the tip of your tongue — literally! One of the best ways to change the way you think about something is to start speaking differently. When you speak positively about your life, you reinforce positive mindsets and therefore generate positive feelings, which in turn lead to positive actions that have a positive impact on your life. Your words then become a self-fulfilling prophecy.

Start building a millionaire mindset today simply by starting to speak positively about yourself and your world.

If negative words have brought you down or held you back in the past, change that by neutralising the power of those words. If someone has told you you're no good, start by telling yourself what a great person you are. If you've been told that you'll never make it, start telling yourself that you *are* going to make it, that it *can* be done and you are *going* to do it. If you've been told that you're just average, start telling yourself that you are outstanding.

> If someone has told you you're no good, start by telling yourself what a great person you are.

If there are things in your world that you want to change, start talking about those things as though they are changing.

If both death and life are in the power of the tongue, then it's up to you to make the choice. My advice to you is to choose life!

Challenge:
Watch your mouth

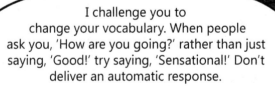

I challenge you to change your vocabulary. When people ask you, 'How are you going?' rather than just saying, 'Good!' try saying, 'Sensational!' Don't deliver an automatic response.

You cannot speak positively about someone and then have a negative feeling about them. And you can't think negatively about money, prosperity or abundance and then feel good about it. Watch your words.

Become a top shelf person

America has blessed many nations with great franchises. One of the incredible franchises that has been shipped to the shores of many nations — including Australia — is the great Krispy Kreme Doughnuts franchise. The reason I love Krispy Kreme doughnuts is because they are the only low calorie doughnut in the world … not! But seriously, I love Krispy Kreme doughnuts and every chance I get to eat them, I'm in.

There is a Krispy Kreme franchise at Sydney Airport. In my line of work I travel a lot and I'm regularly passing through there. Generally I leave for the airport about 45 minutes earlier than necessary, just in case my plane leaves early — at least that's what I tell my wife. The real reason I get to the airport early is so I can enjoy a Krispy Kreme doughnut and a cup of coffee.

One day I was at a Krispy Kreme store and there was a guy there with his two little girls. I was standing in line behind them waiting to be served. The girls were looking in eager anticipation at all the choices available in the doughnut cabinet. Watching these cute little girls made me feel a little wistful because they reminded me of my own two daughters when they were little.

As I was admiring this charming little scene unfold in front of me, I heard the father say to his daughters, 'Girls, you can have any doughnuts you like, except for the ones on the top shelf.' Now, you and I know that the doughnuts those little girls wanted were — you guessed it — on the top shelf!

On the top shelf were the most expensive doughnuts, but they were only about 20 or 30 cents more than the other doughnuts. I could see these two little girls eagerly looking at the top shelf doughnuts. They were obviously disappointed at the news that the top shelf was off-limits.

I quietly went over to the father and handed him $20. (I tried to make sure that I did it in such a way that it would not embarrass him.)

'I teach people to prosper,' I said. 'I encourage people to invest not just in things, but in memories. It's the greatest thing you can give your children. Buy the girls a doughnut from the top shelf. An extra 30 cents isn't going to make you broke.'

This man did not have a millionaire mindset. He had a poverty mindset that made him automatically think, *I can't afford the most expensive doughnuts.* And by telling his daughters that they couldn't have the doughnuts on the top shelf, he was indoctrinating them with the same mindset. Even worse is the possibility that these two delightful little girls could have gone away from that shop thinking, *We don't deserve the best. We're not good enough to have really nice things. We have to settle for second best.* Even something as simple as buying a doughnut can have a critical impact on the mindset of our children.

The problem here was not the doughnuts. The problem was a mindset. How did I know that it was a mindset issue and not a case of genuinely not having enough money? Well, to begin with, I noticed that the man held a packet of cigarettes. Cigarettes cost about $10 a packet and he probably smoked a packet a day—that's about $70 a week or $3640 a year. Even if he was only smoking a couple of packets a week, it's still a lot of money compared to the few cents it would have cost him for a couple of 'top shelf' doughnuts.

This father had a choice: he could invest in mind viruses or he could invest in memories. He could create a mindset in his daughters that would potentially limit their future prosperity or he could begin to build a mindset in them by which they would grow up believing that they have unlimited potential. He could spend his money on cigarettes and watch it go up in smoke or he could invest his small change in the future prosperity of his two delightful little children.

After the man ordered and paid for his 'top shelf' doughnuts, one of the little girls looked at me and smiled. 'Thanks, mister,' she said. Personally, I'd pay $20 to see a smile like that any day!

Come up a level

Several years ago I was attending a conference, and with me was one of my mentors, a gentleman who is a very successful entrepreneur and who owns arguably one of the largest franchises in Australia. We were at a menswear store and a beautiful tie caught my eye. Now, I like nice ties.

So often we settle for less than what we want...

The price tag was $190 and yet I thought to myself, *I really want that tie!* The problem was that I had never before spent more than $20 on a tie, so the price was a stretch. Then, out of the corner of my eye I saw another great tie. On closer examination I noticed it had a price tag of $90. *That is a lot of money for a tie,* I thought to myself. *I could settle for the $90 tie and save $100.*

Noticing that I was vacillating between the two ties, my friend said, 'Pat, which tie do you really like?'

'I really like the $190 one,' I replied.

'But you're about to purchase the $90 one. It's only $100 more. Stretch yourself. Come up a level.'

My friend challenged my mindset. So often we settle for less than what we want and we believe it's because of a price tag.

In my case, my decision had nothing to do with the price, it had everything to do with what I really wanted and what I felt most comfortable with. If I had bought that $90 tie, I probably would have walked out of that shop thinking, *It was only $100 less than the other one. I should have bought the $190 tie.*

Prosperous people don't spend money ad hoc. They learn to spend money on things that will develop good memories or have a lasting impact. My friend taught me a lesson that day. He taught me that $100 over the longevity of my life isn't that big a deal. So many of us would have settled for the cheaper option—whether it's a meal or an item of clothing. In reality, we are not going to miss the price difference over the long term.

We are born to live a wonderful life! We are meant to advance!

When contemplating a purchase, does your mind naturally go to a 'can't afford it' or a 'too expensive' mindset? A friend of mine who is quite wealthy was once shopping for a ring for his wife. He was accompanied by one of his mentors. He saw a stunning ring priced at $26000 and considered buying it. Although he could easily afford it, he decided that this was too much to pay for a ring. 'I don't need to spend that much,' he reasoned. 'My wife will still be impressed by a much less expensive ring.'

His mentor looked at him and said, 'She may not know the difference, but you will! So stay average then.' He could see that my friend had a mindset issue that needed to be challenged. Despite his affluence, he was retreating into a poverty mindset. It's not a matter of how much money you do or do not have, it's about whether or not you have a millionaire mindset.

What kind of mindset do you have when it comes to wealth, money and prosperity? Do you have a millionaire mindset or a poverty mindset? Are you a 'top shelf' kind of person or a 'bottom shelf' kind of person? Is prosperity something that only happens to other people? Is prosperity something you'd love to have, but can only dream about?

The word 'prosperity' is derived from the Latin word *prosperare*, which means 'to succeed'. The word 'prosper' means 'to be fortunate, to bloom, to flourish, to progress, to succeed and to thrive'. To me, prosperity means wealth, wellbeing, affluence, influence, success and a good life. The connotation of advancement is in all these meanings. My belief is that every one of us is meant to enjoy a prosperous life. We were never meant to only exist. We are born to live a wonderful life! We are meant to advance!

Challenge:
Expand yourself inch by inch

It's okay to eat from the top shelf. Now, you don't have to go for the top shelf all the time. I'm not suggesting that every time you make a purchase that you get into debt. Not at all! Simply learn to grow. Take it gradually—it's a process. Every so often when you buy something, go up a notch; stretch yourself a little bit.

When you next go out for dinner, book a table at a restaurant that's just a little nicer than the ones you've been to before. Make the sacrifice and enjoy it.

Chapter 4

Developing a millionaire mindset

Developing a millionaire mindset means increasing the capacity of your thinking. As William Arthur Ward once said, 'Nothing limits achievement like small thinking; nothing expands possibilities like unleashed thinking.' The only limitations on your mind are the ones you put on it yourself.

We need to be vigilant in not allowing other people to project wrong thoughts and mindsets onto us. People often take on another person's thinking patterns and mindsets without ever really considering whether the mindsets they are adopting are constructive. For example, a person experiencing a marriage crisis may go to a friend for advice, but there may be a problem if that friend has had three failed marriages herself; her thinking and mindset about marriage may not be the most helpful!

Long-term mindsets develop as a result of the way in which we respond to individual experiences and situations. The experience itself is not the real issue. What really matters is how we respond to it. Two people can have very similar experiences, but respond very differently and, as a result, they can each develop very different mindsets. For example, two people might go out, get drunk and later regret it. So they both have a similar experience.

One of them responds by deciding never to get drunk again, declaring, 'What a waste! How could I have done that to myself? I am better than that.' The other person thinks, *Looks like I'm never going to be able to break this cycle.*

The first person's response develops an overcoming mindset that puts him in charge of his life. The second person's response develops a defeatist mindset that makes him a slave to habit. How you perceive your experiences and respond to your experiences will determine how you live in the long run.

Nobody here wears shoes!

There is a story of two shoe salesmen who go to Africa. One of them quickly writes back to his employer, 'Please send me a ticket home. I have no hope of selling shoes here because nobody here wears shoes.'

The other salesman also writes home: 'Please send me a thousand pairs of shoes as soon as you can. There is a great opportunity for us because nobody here wears shoes!' They share the same experience, but they have two different responses. Why? Because they think differently; they have different mindsets.

A few years ago a young man from my recovery centre came to visit me. 'Pat,' he said, 'I suppose I'll always be a recovering drug addict. Nobody will ever want to employ a recovering drug addict. Nobody will ever want to marry someone like me.' It was obvious that this young man had a problem seeing himself as anything other than a drug addict.

I looked him in the eye and said, 'Son, where your focus is today, your future is tomorrow. Life is going to move towards your predominant thought. So Danny, I never want to hear you say, "I'm a recovering drug addict." From today I want you to change your mind and start saying, "I'm a wholesome young man. I'm a good young man. I'm the kind of guy every young woman wants to marry".'

He said to me, 'Pat, why would I not want to say that I'm a recovering drug addict?'

I said to him, 'Danny, nobody ever looks at a butterfly and says, "That's a recovering caterpillar." Neither do they say, "Man, that used to be an ugly caterpillar!" A caterpillar goes through a metamorphosis, a transformation, a period of incubation and it changes. That which was ugly becomes beautiful. Danny, that's what I want you to think.'

...where your focus is today, your future is tomorrow.

So that's what Danny began to think from that day onwards, and that's what he became—a respected, upstanding, eligible, employable young man.

Another story that will illustrate this point happened a little while ago, when I was conducting a program for young people in the United States. As we were dropping some of them home after the program, a young man began to frantically scream, 'I don't want to go home! Please don't make me go home!'

We sat him down and said, 'Jason, you've got to go home. We have a responsibility to take you home after the program.'

Then he lifted up his shirt and, to my shock and disgust, he showed me where his mother's boyfriend had taken a boning knife and carved his name into Jason's skin. He looked at me in anger and frustration and said, 'One day, when I get bigger and stronger, I'm going to kill that man!'

I said to him, 'Jason, everything in your eyes, in your mindset and in your environment tells me you will grow up and achieve that goal. Let me change your mind. You can grow up and do that, but you'll end up in prison. Or, if you listen to what I say, we'll get you out of this environment, get you a good education and surround you with a different level of thinking. You can grow up and study and put men like that behind prison walls.'

Today, Jason is an outstanding young attorney doing incredible work. What changed his mind? What changed his future? It all starts in your thinking. You decide whether you live in a prison or a palace — it all begins with your mindset.

Copy the tall poppies, don't cut them down

In Australia we have what we call the 'tall poppy syndrome.' People with a tall poppy syndrome want to cut successful people down to size; it is a euphemism for a poverty mindset. People with a poverty mindset hate the idea that others may be more successful than they are. Instead of looking for mentors, all they want to do is tear down people who have achieved wealth and prosperity. On the other hand, a millionaire mindset makes wealthy people mentors, not villains.

So how do you change the way you think?

The big question, of course, is how do you go about changing the way you think? One strategy you can adopt is a therapeutic technique called the 'miracle question':

Imagine when you go to bed tonight that while you are asleep a miracle happens — your world becomes perfect. You now have ideal relationships. You now have your ideal job. You are now your ideal weight. You now have the ideal house. But the deal is this: you can't tell your friends and family about the miracle and the only way to keep the miracle going is to continue to live it out.

This technique is designed to help you to begin thinking differently about your life. So, how would you respond to this miracle? How would you act, speak and think so that the miracle continues? Well then, from this point onwards in your own life, why don't you go ahead and act, speak and think exactly like that! Live it out. Start thinking and acting as though things *have* changed today. Again, it's like the thermometer–thermostat analogy: instead of your thoughts and actions reacting to your external environment like a thermometer, set your mental thermostat so that it changes your external environment.

We need to recognise thought habits that are...wrong and change them.

Your actions are determined by your thought patterns. When you think a certain way, you will act accordingly. Often we are not conscious of how our thinking determines our behaviour because we have developed thought patterns that have become habitual. We need to recognise thought habits that are non-productive, ineffective, dysfunctional or wrong and change them.

When someone is in a bad mood, we often describe it by saying, 'They got up on the wrong side of the bed!' We say this as if all it takes to change a bad mood is to swap the side of the bed we sleep on. A person who is in a bad mood has often succumbed to a habit of thinking that has affected that person in a negative way. That person needs to become aware of their mood and make a decision to change their mindset.

Developing a millionaire mindset

There are a number of things you can do to develop a millionaire mindset. Here are four basic strategies:

1. *RENEW your mind.* The cells in your body are constantly regenerating. You need to do the same with your mind. You need to be proactive in depositing new, positive thoughts into your mind every day.

2. *REPLACE old mindsets.* When something you own is no longer serving you well, what do you do? You get a new one! It's the same with mindsets. If the mindset you have today is not going to get you to where you want to go in life, get a new one. Trade in your old mindset for a millionaire mindset. Even the most positive thoughts you have will be short-lived if you hold on to negative mindsets. If you don't actually change your old thinking habits or patterns, then the positive thought will soon be overpowered. Replace old mindsets with new patterns of thinking.

   For example, if your mindset about marriage is that it is a drag, then even the best marriage seminar in the world isn't going to be enough to change your attitude. You need to develop a mindset that says, 'Marriage is great! I love being married! I love the person I'm married to!' It's about putting in the effort required to replace old mindsets with new ones.

3. *REALIGN your thinking.* Regularly ask yourself, *Is this the right way to think?* Become a little introspective; think about your thinking. When you find yourself acting in a way that is not conducive to increasing your prosperity, ask yourself, *Why am I acting like this?*

What's going on in my head right now? What mindset is causing me to behave in this way? How should I be thinking? What needs to change in my head?

4. *RE-ESTABLISH your convictions.* Some things in life are a matter of preference, but others are a matter of conviction. A preference is usually something we can take up or leave behind. I might prefer chocolate ice-cream to vanilla, but if there's no chocolate left I'm not going to lose any sleep over it. But when something is a matter of conviction, it becomes non-negotiable. A conviction is not a thought you possess, it is a thought that possesses you. Convictions are the things that people are prepared to make great sacrifices for. Some people even die for their convictions. What convictions drive your life? Are your convictions propelling you forward into a life of success and wealth? Is prosperity a preference for you or a conviction? Is prosperity non-negotiable in your life?

Challenge:
Make up your mind to change your mind

Make up your mind to change your mind today. Start thinking bigger. Expand your capacity. Don't let all those bare feet put you off selling more shoes! Begin seeing the world around you as being full of opportunity, rather than impossibility. That's a millionaire mindset!

Chapter 5

Climbing the walls in your mind

People may have scaled lofty mountains and climbed the highest peaks, but the biggest obstacles that people struggle to climb over and the tallest mountains people attempt to conquer are the wrong mindsets handed to us from our parents, our culture and our upbringing. You won't be able to reach your dreams if you haven't first scaled the walls that confine you in your mind.

Negative mindsets can come from a wide range of sources. Perhaps at some time in your life someone labeled you a 'failure', a 'loser', a 'no-hoper' or an 'underachiever.' Labels such as these can create negative mindsets about ourselves. We need to reject such labels and not allow them to gain power over our minds.

Have you ever had a teacher or sports coach say to you statements like: 'You'll never amount to much!', 'You don't have what it takes!', or 'You'll always be average'? Statements such as these can have a powerful influence on the way you think about yourself. Refuse to accept them.

Another source of negative mindsets can be our upbringing. Parents and family are typically our earliest role models and we tend to take on their worldviews without realising it. What kind of upbringing did you have? Were you encouraged to think big and dream big? Or were you taught not to expect much from life? Were you encouraged to stand out from the crowd and believe in yourself? Or were you told not to make a fuss and to just try and blend in with the crowd? Did your upbringing provide you with positive role models for your relationships? Or were all your relationship models dysfunctional?

You need to be able to identify any negative mindsets that may have been set during your upbringing. You need to understand where they came from so that you can deal with them. Your greatest war is fought in your mind; it's where the greatest battles are won and lost.

> ...understand where [negative mindsets come] from so that you can deal with them.

If you can't climb the walls ...

Unfortunately in my work I have come across people who have been unable to scale the walls that are keeping their minds and their lives confined. One of my greatest joys in life is speaking to students in high schools. I speak to 100 000 high-school students every year free of charge and try to motivate young people to live lives of excellence and to avoid short-circuiting their destinies.

One particular high school I visited remains impressed in my mind. I noticed there an outstanding young artist who had painted some of the most beautiful pictures of landscapes and portraits I had ever seen. She had won a school award and a cash prize for her work — she was overjoyed. She went home and showed her dad the winning picture and told him about the award she had just received.

But all her father did was criticise the picture and point out its faults.

Some years later I was speaking to an audience of businesspeople and I noticed this same young lady in the audience. Something about her stood out, but it seemed the fire, the passion and the joy had died in her. She invited me back to her house for a coffee and I gladly accepted. When I walked into her house I noticed half a dozen pictures, all half finished. They were beautiful portraits and landscapes, but they weren't complete. I turned to her and said, 'These paintings are so beautiful, and yet you've not finished one!'

She looked at me and said, 'Pat, the reason why I have not finished them is that nobody can criticise an unfinished work.'

Sadly, her father had planted a seed in her young mind that said, 'Whatever you do is not good enough!'

Many years ago I had the opportunity to build one of Australia's largest youth organisations. Around that same time I was involved in a church ministry. As a result of our work we were able to help some of the most dysfunctional young people on the planet to find hope and faith. One particular young lady who came into our church community at that time was as pretty as a picture, but she had no boundaries in her life and she often dressed far too inappropriately. Nonetheless, we loved her and received her and never judged her.

She soon found work at a local restaurant and my kids and I would visit her there sometimes. We were so pleased to see her blossom and grow in life. Her outside appearance didn't change, but her inside sure did.

Someone I would describe as a religious nut approached her one day and asked, 'Are you a believer?'

'Yes, I am!' she said. 'I'm a friend of Pat's. He brought me to church.'

He said to her, 'Well you don't dress like one. You look like a street worker.'

She came up to me and was so embarrassed. In fact, she was more worried about the embarrassment she had caused me than her own sense of self-esteem. When she told me what had happened, I quickly apologised and reassured her of our love for her and acceptance of her. I told her that we did not judge her and that we loved her just the way she was. I told her she was a wonderful young lady with a great future.

Needless to say, I didn't see her again until a few years later, when I was on the Gold Coast to speak to a room full of people. I was about to get up and speak when I noticed out of the corner of my eye a group of rather attractive young ladies who had dressed themselves to be noticed. I took one glance and knew immediately that they were call girls. I pointed these ladies out to one of my friends and said, 'I believe they're escorts.'

> Don't let other peoples' negative words become planted in your mind.

That night I talked about how hurts can lead to bitterness in our lives. Immediately after the meeting these young women rushed up to me and one of the ladies said, 'Pat, do you remember me?'

'No,' I said, rather embarrassed. 'I don't remember you.'

She said, 'I'm Madeleine. I used to come to your church.'

I asked her what she was doing for a living and she hung her head. Tears ran down her cheeks as she said, 'Well, I normally tell people I'm a waitress, but I can't lie to you, Pat. I'm actually a callgirl.'

At that point I realised she had become the fruit of a seed someone in my church had planted in her mind some years before. Fortunately, some friends and I were able to take Madeleine out of that situation and we saw her life change for the better.

Don't let other peoples' negative words become planted in your mind. People may tell you, 'You won't amount to much!' or 'You're a loser!' or 'You'll never make it!' Those words have the potential to become embedded in your subconscious, where they can produce fruit that you do not want on the tree of your life.

You've got to make up your mind to shift your thinking. If you don't make up your mind, your mind will make up its mind for you. You've got to climb those walls and get your thinking to another level.

Climb those walls by becoming a 'master asker'

My two daughters have been brought up with a prosperity mindset. Other people are brought up without a prosperity mentality. Interestingly, two people can have very similar upbringings, but develop very different mindsets.

I know of two brothers who developed two very different mindsets, despite sharing the same upbringing. One grew up thinking his father was a tightwad, while the other never thought of his father as anything but generous. In actual fact, the father treated both sons the same, but because they each had a different mindset about their father, they had different perceptions of his behaviour towards them. One reality, but two different mindsets resulted in different perceptions of that reality. Your mindset has a powerful influence over how you perceive and experience reality.

I have no recollection of my father denying me anything. I never had a problem asking him for anything. Some people grow up with strong, controlling personalities and develop a fear of asking for things. They feel nervous going to the boss to ask for a raise. I've learnt to be a 'master asker' — I'm not afraid to ask.

To have a millionaire mindset, you need to become a master asker. This will help you to climb the walls that are currently keeping you confined. You need to know:

- *when to ask.* Timing is important. There's a right time to ask and a wrong time to ask. Wait until all the circumstances are most favourable, then ask.

- *what to ask for.* Know exactly what it is you want. Don't ask for one thing when what you really need is something else. For example, don't ask for advice when what you really need is information; don't ask for a loan when what you really need is a donation; don't ask for 'a minute of your time' when you really need a couple of hours. Be accurate in what you ask for and be specific.

- *how to ask.* Learn the art of persuasion. Think about the best way to approach the person you want something from and be diplomatic. I'm not talking about manipulation, flattery or deceit. It's a matter of using some common sense and wisdom and knowing the best way to go about asking in order to get a positive response.

- *who to ask.* Don't ask just anybody. If you need investment advice, you won't ask your mechanic. If your car needs fixing, you won't take it to your dentist. If you need money, don't ask someone who doesn't have any. Figure out exactly what you need, then decide who would be the best person to ask for help.

- *why that person will want to give you what you need.*
  Before you ask, make sure you know why it is in that person's interest to give you what you're asking for. Know the answer to the question, 'Why should I help you?' Make sure you understand what's in it for them.

As children, many of us asked for things and were told, 'No, we can't afford that! Do you think money grows on trees? Do you think I'm made of money?' Constantly hearing these answers creates a blueprint for your life. From then on, your expectation is that if you ask for anything, the answer will always be, 'No!' From then on, every time you want to ask for something, you may stop and think, 'So what's the point of asking?'

We need to create a positive environment around our minds and not be trapped inside walls that hold us back. Things thrive in the environment to which they are suited. To be prosperous, you need to create an environment that supports prosperity. If you have negative mindsets about things like wealth, prosperity and success, you need to be coached and trained to change your way of thinking.

To have a millionaire mindset, you need to become a master asker.

Really, they're not thinking about you ...

Sometimes we are brought up with certain belief systems that we commit to because we're worried about what people would think if we didn't. This is a wall that people often have trouble overcoming. The truth is, other people don't think about you that often!

I was once doing some individual coaching with a client who was one of the top real estate agents in New Zealand. She said, 'Pat, I know I could get to another level if I just stopped worrying about what other people think of me.'

I said to her, 'You know, they don't think of you that often.' And it was like a light went on in her head. I then said, 'You play ping-pong in your head all day. "What will they think? What should I do?" In fact, I predict that right now you are in a state of indecision.'

'You're right.' she said, astonished. 'This morning I was discussing whether or not to go to a party tonight with my husband. I really want to go and he wants to go, but we're so worried about these other people being there and how we're going to have a terrible time—'

I interrupted her: 'Why are you allowing someone else to dictate whether or not you have fun and do what you want to do? Make a decision and stick to it.'

'Okay, we're going to the party and we're going to have a damn good time!' she said defiantly.

She had stopped playing mental ping-pong. She called her husband right away and told him they were going to the party.

En route to success, the road is full of ups and downs

The millionaire mindset doesn't play mental ping-pong, repeatedly tossing a decision back and forward, never to make any progress. If anything, the millionaire mindset plays mental golf—always moving forward, aiming for a specific point ahead, trying to take the most direct path possible. Of course, the most direct path is rarely the path you will take.

En route to success, the ground is not usually flat, but full of ups and downs; there are usually one or two rough patches you have to find your way out of; there are always a few traps to be avoided; and occasionally you might find the water and have to play your shot again. But while your shots might not always go according to plan, no matter what happens, you always continue to move forward with your end point in mind, even if it's not always in sight!

Your inability to decide to move on—your inability to put off an old mindset to take on a new one—will hinder your prosperity. Imagine what you would look like if you got out of bed every day and put clean clothes over your old clothes. Firstly, you'd look ridiculous. And secondly, you'd smell terrible. Similarly, if you want to put on a new mindset, first you've got to take off the old one. If you want to put on a new set of values, you've first got to get rid of the old ones; you have to erase the bad content first before you put in new, improved content.

> You will either make money or excuses, but you cannot do both.

The dog ate my homework

Another obstacle that preserves negative mindsets and keeps people trapped in their lives is excuses. You will either make money or excuses, but you cannot do both. Excuses are the means by which we attempt to justify our shortcomings. Excuses are ammunition we use against ourselves in acts of self-sabotage. Blame is a type of excuse. Some people are constantly looking for reasons why things are not working for them, so they blame it on their lack of progress and prosperity. They blame the stock market, they blame the product, they blame their colleagues and they blame the boss. Sometimes they blame things such as their past or their upbringing.

Ultimately, these are no more than paltry excuses that people use to justify a lack of vision and a lack of capacity for increased prosperity. The truth is, it's your choice. You can choose excuses or a millionaire mindset—you can't have both.

When you find a reason, you'll find a way

People make excuses for all sorts of things. Some people make excuses for being overweight. They say things like 'I've had five children,' or, 'I was a big child.' Others make excuses based on their past. They might say, 'I was brought up in a dysfunctional home.' Still others use lack of knowledge as an excuse. These people say, 'I was never taught that.'

> The moment you seek to excuse yourself, you sabotage your advancement.

At the end of the day, my response to such excuses is, 'So what?' The moment you seek to excuse yourself, you sabotage your advancement. Everyone has stuff they have to deal with. So what's the big deal? It's not like we've all taken a pill to inoculate us against pain. Instead of using excuses for our lack of advancement, we need to ask ourselves the question, 'What am I going to do about it?' Stop using excuses and start finding reasons why you *can* move ahead.

Recently, a woman in one of my mentoring groups said to me, 'I am always late for work.'

I asked her why this was and she replied, 'I don't really know. I always *try* to get to work on time,' she said.

'That's your problem,' I told her. 'You are trying to get to work *on time*, so you get up at a certain hour, but most things generally take more time than you allow. Don't try to get to work on time, try to get there *early*. Then you may arrive on time.'

She was looking for an excuse for being late; I helped her find a reason she could arrive on time.

Similarly, tennis great Virginia Wade played at Wimbledon for 15 years straight without ever winning the title. Several other wins at the US Open and the Australian Open were not able to fill the gap left by so many winless Wimbledons. Wade had got caught up in making excuses — bad luck, bad weather, poor line calls, bad bounces — she found all kinds of excuses to explain her failure to win a Wimbledon title.

Then, in 1977, Virginia Wade adopted a more proactive approach to her tennis. She gave up making excuses and committed herself to winning at Wimbledon. No matter what circumstances were in front of her, she refused to make any more excuses. She took personal responsibility for her own mistakes, the quality of her game and her competitive spirit (or lack thereof). Virginia Wade won her first Wimbledon championship in 1977.

Nobody is a real loser — until they start blaming somebody else

John Wooden was one of the greatest basketball coaches of all time. He led his team, the UCLA Bruins, to a record-breaking number of NCAA basketball championships and gained the respect of players and spectators alike. He was inspirational — he led and propelled his teams to many great victories. He always admonished his players to take responsibility for their actions. One of his memorable motivational statements was this: 'Nobody is a real loser — until they start blaming somebody else.'

Are you in the habit of making excuses? If you are, stop it! You were designed for advancement, you were engineered for prosperity and you have been endowed with seeds of greatness. Excuses short-circuit your destiny and create the opposite kind of life to the one you are meant to have. Broke people make excuses; people with a millionaire mindset make a life. No more excuses!

With prosperity comes a certain amount of responsibility that cannot be excused. The ability to accept this responsibility is the measure of a person. Your capacity to accept responsibility for your own prosperity is the measure of how much of it will come to you. Unfortunately, some people recognise responsibility only to avoid it. They are always busy doing something other than what they should be doing because it is easier and allows them to avoid responsibility. The millionaire mindset, however, does not dodge responsibility; it faces it head on and acts upon it. Responsibility creates within us a capacity for greater wealth and prosperity.

> Broke people make excuses; people with a millionaire mindset make a life.

'I never let my schooling interfere with my education.'

One final wall that I want to address here is this: some people think that you have to be educated to be able to become wealthy. This is just not true! Education does not equal wealth.

I have met countless highly educated people who are unable to live successful and prosperous lives. At the same time, all over the world there are high school dropouts who have been very successful — people like Bill Gates, Thomas Edison, Federico Fellini and Steve Jobs. William Feather, author of *The Business of Life*, made this remark: 'Two delusions fostered by higher education are that what is taught corresponds to what is learned, and that it will somehow pay off in money.'

Mark Twain put it aptly when he said, 'I never let my schooling interfere with my education.' Remember, you do not have to be educated, you just have to think with a millionaire mindset.

Challenge:
Expect great results

Develop positive expectations. *Expect* things to go well, *expect* yourself to prosper, *expect* to be wealthy, *expect* to be on time, *expect* to be healthy and *expect* to develop great friendships. Positive expectation is the breeding ground for miracles.

I have found that whatever you focus your attention on will grow. If you focus your attention on making excuses, then your excuses will flourish. If you focus on creating wealth, then that will expand. If you spend your mental energy on constantly worrying, excusing and justifying, it will be difficult—if not impossible, to create abundance in your life.

Determine to focus on your success, expect wealth, rid your life of all excuses and you will begin to see great results!

Chapter 6

Developing a healthy view of yourself

A critical factor in developing a millionaire mindset is to develop a healthy view of yourself. How do you see yourself? Do you see yourself as a person who deserves to prosper? Do you see yourself someone with the potential and the ability to become prosperous? Or do you feel unworthy of prosperity? Perhaps you think that prosperity is beyond you, that you don't have what it takes. Sterling W Sill said this: 'Wealth is not only what you have, but it is also what you are.'

The reason many people don't prosper is not because of their lack of ability or their circumstances, but who they think or feel they are and how they see themselves. The level of prosperity in your life will be determined to a large extent by who you are as a person.

To be prosperous, you need to have a clear picture of the person you believe you can be. You will naturally gravitate towards the dominant image of yourself in your mind. If thoughts of anxiety are your dominant mindset, then you'll gravitate towards anxiety. It's like trying to hit a dartboard with a dart when you're facing another direction. To hit a target you must be facing the direction of the target — and focusing on it.

Many people get into a rut with their thinking. They don't believe they deserve to prosper. They think increased prosperity will never happen. Remember, the only difference between a rut and a grave is time. Don't die with prosperity sitting dormant within you!

Don't die with prosperity sitting dormant within you!

You need to learn to think like this: who deserves nice things? I do! Who deserves a prosperous family? I do! Who deserves a nice home? I do! Who deserves to wear nice clothes? I do! Who deserves to have a life that is advancing with wealth and increase? I do! You *deserve* these things!

The biggest hindrance to prosperity is not a lack of money, it's a wrong mindset. Change how you see yourself and others. Your life will not advance until your mind is set to advance. Your view of wealth is wealth's view of you.

Looking in the mirror

When you look at yourself, what do you see? Whatever self-image you have is what you will subconsciously work towards — they become self-fulfilling prophecies. You cannot have two competing thoughts at once — one thought will always dominate. If you are thinking you'd love to be more prosperous, but your dominant mentality about yourself is 'I'm not worth much,' or 'I don't deserve prosperity,' then you will never be truly successful.

As I told you earlier, I once bought a beautiful silk tie for $190. When I told a friend how much it had cost me, he was absolutely shocked that I would spend so much on a tie; he had a mind virus about spending money on clothes. But to me, that tie was not an extravagant purchase. In my role as a public speaker I want to look good and feel good about myself. I cannot stand in front of people and challenge them to develop the mindset of a millionaire if I'm not practising what I preach. I dress according to the image that I want to project. I dress according to what I think I am worth. I perceive value in myself. Rather than thinking, *That's too much to pay for a tie!* I prefer to think, *I deserve to wear a tie like that! I'm worth it! When you think about it, silk is really just expensive worm poo. Why am I not good enough to wear that?*

You see, it's not about being conceited or arrogant or narcissistic, it's about valuing yourself and developing freer attitudes about money, wealth and prosperity.

You've heard of the fairytale *Snow White and the Seven Dwarfs*, for example. In that classic tale the vain queen asks her magic mirror, 'Mirror, mirror on the wall, who is the fairest of them all?'

Each time, the mirror answers, 'Snow White is the fairest one of all.' I hold to the belief that it is impossible to avoid the outer manifestation of your inner view of yourself. In other words, you will live out how you see yourself. Your net worth is linked to your self-worth.

If you are reading this book and thinking, *I really would like to be prosperous, but I don't believe I have the energy and focus needed to become a prosperous person,* then you have two competing thoughts in your mind. At some point one of them will overcome the other. If, on the one hand, you desire prosperity, and yet on the other hand your mindset is one in which you are lacking, then this negative mindset will dominate your self-image. Until you see yourself as a person who has the capacity to be prosperous, prosperity will continue to elude you.

In which direction are you going?

Perspective is so important to prosperity. Life impacts us all in so many different ways that each of us has developed our own unique perspectives. For example, when you stand on top of a mountain, the direction you face determines your perspective. Where you stand determines what you see. When you face north, you get a northern perspective. When you face south, you get a southern perspective; we can see many different perspectives from the same mountain.

A millionaire mindset places a high value on self...

I've known people who have been involved in identical businesses, and yet one has succeeded while the other one has failed! The bottom line is this: the difference is their perspectives.

Have you ever given yourself permission to prosper? To feel good about feeling good — you should try walking around with a sign saying, 'Pardon me, I'm prospering!' Tragically, some people are so good to others, but very bad to themselves. Eventually, that won't last.

How much are you worth?

How do you see yourself? Until you learn to value yourself properly, you will not be able to develop a millionaire mindset. Why? You will lack the motivation needed to pursue a life of true prosperity.

'But...' I hear you ask, 'isn't it really more important to value other people? Shouldn't my motivation to be wealthy stem from a desire to help others?' Yes, but you should value yourself above others. Consider this principle of the Christian faith: love your neighbour as yourself. This implies that you can only love your neighbour if you first love *yourself*. It's true — how in the world can you love someone else if you don't love yourself? A millionaire mindset places a high value on self and then turns that outward by placing equally high value on other people.

The two greatest motivators are recognition and reward

To illustrate this, let me tell you a bit about myself. When I was a child, my family didn't have much. I wanted desperately to earn some money. So at the age of 10 I went and got my first job. Now, the Sydney suburb of Bankstown was not exactly thriving — in fact, it was one of the worst suburbs in Sydney at that time. Back then it experienced a lot of economic problems, but it was a community to which a lot of Lebanese, Greeks and Italians migrated. My own family migrated there from Italy. In fact, at school we used to play a game called 'Spot the Aussie'!

I got my first job at a fruit and vegetable market in Bankstown. I remember I used to earn 40 cents an hour packing potatoes into plastic bags. I became so good at packing potatoes that I was soon promoted to packing onions as well.

Across the road was another fruit and vegetable shop owned by a man named Peter. Peter had heard of my skills as a potato packer and then as an onion packer. My fame had spread throughout the Bankstown fruit market community. There I was, the potato packer champion of Bankstown! (I may be short, but I've got very fast hands!)

Peter 'headhunted' me. Instead of offering me 40 cents an hour, he told me he would give me 10 cents a bag.

I immediately realised that my value was increasing. My perspective began to change. I began to see myself as the fastest potato packer in Bankstown because I was now paid by the bag, not by the hour. Reward is a great motivator; my productivity increased because the value I placed on myself increased.

Some years later, as a high school student I wanted to buy a guitar, so my dad got me a job at Victa Lawn Mowers. I worked on the assembly line and I was paid about $3 to $4 an hour. Years later I took on a position working with youth in a local church. I was paid the huge sum of $140 a week! I realised that I would have to supplement my income, so I went back to the fruit market — this time it was the Flemington Fruit Market. I didn't realise how much the fame of my childhood exploits had spread throughout the fruit market community in Sydney, but when I walked in on the first day of my job people stared at me in absolute awe. They began to say, 'It's him! He's no taller than he was, but he looks older!' They asked me, 'Is it you?'

'Yes, it is me,' I replied. 'Pat Mesiti, the fastest potato packer in Bankstown!'

So I went to work every day, starting at 4 am and working until 10 am to supplement my income. Now, fast forward to 2005. I recently flew to Europe to speak and I was paid $10 000 an hour. What's changed? I'm the same person, same height, same name and same looks. What has changed is my value to the marketplace.

The other week I was offered a huge sum of money to do some work for a company. My first reaction was: why would they call me? Then it dawned on me — of course they would call me! Who else would they call? You see, it's the value I bring to people and to organisations that quantifies what I earn.

Net worth is related to self-worth

Your net worth is directly related to your self-worth. If you work on yourself, your value will grow. Many people think they are paid for their time, but they're not—they're paid for their value.

People have tried to stick a mind virus in me, telling me, 'You can't make that much money! You're just a Bankstown boy! You'll always be a Bankstown boy. You can take the boy out of Bankstown, but you can't take Bankstown out of the boy.' Well, I really believe you can. You can change if you choose to—change starts with your mindset and you've got to start today.

Challenge:
Realise your true worth

What value do you place on your mind and your knowledge? Do you baulk at the cost of attending a seminar that might help you improve your mind? If you truly value yourself, you won't think twice about spending money on self-improvement. A negative mindset will say, 'That's a luxury I can't justify!' A positive and healthy mindset will say, 'I am worth it!'

To develop a millionaire mindset, you need to see yourself in a new light. If you've always thought of yourself as a pauper, start seeing yourself as a prince. If you don't value yourself as much as you should, then start to speak differently about yourself and act differently towards yourself. Give yourself a treat. Tell yourself that you deserve it and that you are worth it.

Chapter 7

The 10 key characteristics of a millionaire mindset

So far in this book, we've looked at mind viruses that might be holding you back, attitudes that you might need to change, walls to be climbed and behaviours and thought patterns that must be eliminated if you are to reach your goals. Now, here is the part I'm sure you've all been waiting for. We are going to look at the 10 key characteristics of a millionaire mindset.

What makes up a millionaire mindset? How does a wealthy person think? What makes a successful person tick? Well, for a start, people with a millionaire mindset think bigger than others around them. They don't think, *I can't afford a top-shelf doughnut.* They have a mindset of unlimited possibility, which is reflected in their prosperous lives.

But there is so much more to a millionaire mindset. The following are the 10 key characteristics of a millionaire mindset. This list will help you begin to understand the kind of thinking it takes to become a candidate for a life of continually increasing prosperity.

Millionaire mindset characteristic 1: Play to win!

Having a millionaire mindset means you play to win, as opposed to simply playing not to lose. At half time in the 2005 soccer final of the European Champions League, AC Milan had a three–nil lead over Liverpool. Then, in the second half, Liverpool scored three goals in six minutes and went on to win the final in a penalty shootout. AC Milan went from playing to win, to playing to defend their lead — and ended up losing the match. A person with a millionaire mindset always stays on the front foot pushing forward, no matter how far in front they might be. A millionaire mindset plays to advance and to win, not merely to maintain a level or a lead.

Life follows our convictions and our focus, not our desires.

Millionaire mindset characteristic 2: Be inquisitive

A person with a millionaire mindset is a person who is constantly asking questions and finding answers. Unlike the person with a poverty mindset, they don't assume that they already know it all. They are inquisitive, not opinionated.

Rather than being an armchair expert, a prosperity thinker is always learning something new. When they are in conversation with someone who is more knowledgeable about a topic than they are, they don't pretend to know more than they do. Instead, they adopt a learning attitude and defer to the superior knowledge of the other person. They see it as an opportunity to expand their own understanding.

In fact, with a millionaire mindset, every new meeting is treated as an opportunity to learn something new.

Millionaire mindset characteristic 3: Practise selective hearing

The millionaire mindset is able to ignore criticism. I don't listen to my critics; I listen to my mentors and leaders, the people I have given permission to speak into my life. Donald Trump says that he doesn't listen to everybody, only to his 'somebodies.' Successful people tend to be criticised more than anyone else, so to be successful you need to learn to ignore your critics. Criticism usually comes from people who have a poverty mindset. They develop stereotypes of wealthy people and immediately assume that if you are wealthy you must be no good. They say, 'I wonder how many people he had to walk over to get to where he is?' or 'I bet she has never done a hard day's work in her life!'

People who say things like that are really expressing a lacking mindset — a mind virus. Because they don't think of themselves as having the potential to prosper, they resent people who have achieved prosperity.

Millionaire mindset characteristic 4: Progress from desire to commitment

A person with a millionaire mindset goes beyond desire to commitment. It's not enough to *want* to be prosperous — you have to be passionately committed to becoming prosperous. Life follows our convictions and our focus, not our desires. Desire is a starting point, but as long as something remains only in the realm of desire, it is only an option.

When I was head of a drug rehabilitation organisation, there were people who desired to break their addiction. However, unless they were prepared to focus on changing and totally commit to it, their desire was not enough. When we move from the realm of desire to commitment, that which was optional becomes non-negotiable.

Millionaire mindset characteristic 5: Self-worth before net worth

People with a millionaire mindset have a different understanding of their personal worth. They develop their self-worth before they develop their net worth. You can be paid either for your time or for the value you bring to people. A poverty mindset sees time as the primary basis for payment — you work a certain number of hours and get paid on an hourly basis. This means that your level of prosperity is determined by your hourly rate and the amount of time you are able to give to your work.

> People with a millionaire mindset ... develop their self-worth before they develop their net worth.

A person with a millionaire mindset understands that time is irrelevant to prosperity and that wealth is much more about who they are and what they do than how many hours they work.

Millionaire mindset characteristic 6 Learn from the greats, not just the accessible

There are three levels of relationships that you and I need. The first one is your peers — the people with whom you work. The second level is people who are walking behind you, following in your footsteps. The third level is people who are ahead of you — people you look up to.

You will learn from both mistakes and mentors in life. In truth, learning from a mentor is easier. I always challenge people: 'I dare you to catch me without a book in my briefcase! If you do, I'll give you a thousand dollars in cash.' I haven't been caught in 18 years. By constantly reading books, I am regularly being mentored.

To have a millionaire mindset is to recognise the need for mentors, for people you can look up to and from whom you can seek guidance and inspiration. These are people who have been successful and achieved the things that you are still aiming for.

Millionaire mindset characteristic 7: Use what's in your hands to do what's in your heart

A dream in your heart without a plan in your head will never become a reality. Millionaire mindset people use what is in their hand to do what's in their heart. People with a poverty mindset are not driven by what's in their heart and, as a result, their hands are tied. People like Sir Bob Geldof and Bono are passionate about causes such as the elimination of poverty in the world. They have used their celebrity status as rock stars to try to influence world leaders to bring about change, as was evidenced by the Live 8 global rock concert. 'Celebrity is ridiculous,' Bono says. 'It's silly, but it's a kind of currency, and you have to spend it wisely.' He uses what's in his hand to do what's in his heart.

Start by asking yourself what's in your heart. What's your dream? What's your passion? Then ask yourself: 'What do I have in my hand today that I can utilise to start moving in the direction of what's in my heart?' That's a millionaire mindset.

Millionaire mindset characteristic 8: Invest in memories and outcomes

A person with a millionaire mindset uses money to buy memories and outcomes, not just material possessions. One of the great secrets of every successful salesperson is they know that people purchase outcomes. If a lady purchases shoes to go to a ball, she wants an *outcome* — she wants to feel good, which will make her look good so people will notice her.

When someone buys a house, they want an outcome — they want a safe place to raise their family or a good investment. They're not buying a product, they're buying an outcome. When you buy food, you're buying an outcome — nutrition for you and your family. When you purchase a holiday, you're buying an outcome — a memory, something that is intangible, yet powerfully important.

A person with a poverty mindset uses money simply to buy 'things'. Have you ever heard someone say something like this: 'Why would anyone want to spend $5000 on a five-day holiday? Once it's over, you've got nothing to show for it. If I had $5000 I'd buy a new plasma television!' This reflects a poverty mindset that sees money purely as something to be used to buy material possessions.

I remember once being in a poor area of a large city in the UK when I noticed that despite the poverty of the community, every house had a television satellite dish on its roof.

A prosperity mindset is less utilitarian and sees money as a key to an enriched life. Instead of simply spending money on 'stuff', a prosperous person spends money to enhance relationships, to have new experiences, to buy memories and to make life better for other people.

Millionaire mindset characteristic 9: Live off your giving, not your getting

A millionaire mindset recognises the importance of a seed, whereas a person with a poverty mindset is concerned only with the fruit. Everything in life starts as a seed. Something that might look small and insignificant today could be the seed of something that will change the world tomorrow.

Napoleon Hill, author of the seminal book *Think and Grow Rich*, once said, 'The world is full of unfortunate souls who didn't hear opportunity knock at the door because they were down at the convenience store buying lottery tickets.' Such people are trying to generate fruit in their lives without an understanding that fruit is the end result of a process that begins with the planting of a seed. As a result, when a seed of opportunity presents itself, they fail to see its potential.

> A millionaire mindset is looking for acorns, not oak trees.

A person with a millionaire mindset is aware that every day of our lives could be a day of opportunity, a day where there is a seed to be seized and planted. Sometimes the seed is easily missed — seeds by nature are very small; the giant oak tree grows from a tiny acorn. All the potential greatness of the oak tree lies in that acorn. If the acorn is never planted, the tree will never grow. A millionaire mindset is looking for acorns, not oak trees. Is your focus on the size of the tree or on the seed from which the tree grows?

Millionaire mindset characteristic 10: Have guts!

Another important characteristic of the millionaire mindset is the quality of courage. In his book, *The Millionaire Mind*, Thomas J Stanley identifies courage to take financial risks as something most self-made millionaires have in common. Now, Stanley argues that taking risks does not mean gambling. In fact, very few millionaires gamble at all. Here are a few millionaire mindset principles about courage and risk-taking that were revealed by a group of millionaires who were surveyed by Stanley:

- Think of success, not failure. In taking risks, understand what the probable outcomes will be. Then do whatever you can to improve the chance of getting the outcome you desire.

- Believe in yourself and be prepared to work hard. These are two ways of reducing fear and anxiety and bolstering your courage.

- To build belief in yourself, prepare and plan for success, focus on the key issues, and be well organised.

- Playing competitive sports is a good way to develop the mental toughness needed to handle fear. Develop the attitude and discipline of a successful sportsperson. Develop both physical and mental strength — and courage.

- Strong religious faith is an important factor for almost 40 per cent of the millionaires surveyed. Those who have some kind of strong faith exhibit a higher propensity to take financial risks.

Challenge:
Tap into the millionaire mindset

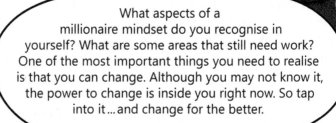

What aspects of a millionaire mindset do you recognise in yourself? What are some areas that still need work? One of the most important things you need to realise is that you can change. Although you may not know it, the power to change is inside you right now. So tap into it…and change for the better.

Chapter 8

Fixing your attitude to money

I have said this before: money is like manure — if you horde it, it stinks, but if you spread it, it makes stuff grow. This is the process for successfully managing the growth of your money: money should be earned, given, invested — and then it should come back to you. Notice that, in that process, *giving* is a key factor to *receiving*.

Why is it that some people prosper, gain wealth, increase their influence and their capacity to do good, invest successfully and manage to leave an inheritance for their children and their children's children, while others struggle? It's largely a matter of your mindset. People can have either a mindset to prosper or a mindset not to prosper. Right thinking will increase your capacity to receive. Wealth is a sign neither of luck nor greed. Most often, it is the result of someone having developed a right mindset and an action plan for their money.

It might seem like an obvious statement, but to develop a millionaire mindset you need to have a positive mindset about money. Some people have some pretty silly ideas when it comes to money. I want to debunk some of those ideas and help you begin to understand what money is really all about. Money would have to be one of the most controversial and misunderstood topics on the planet. We need to shift our mindset and dispel the ridiculous myths about money that have been handed down to us through family, culture, religion or social heritage. Today, you and I need to adopt a new way of thinking about money. We need to have a sound understanding of what money is all about.

Money is just a tool

Money is an incredible tool, but it's a lousy master. As much as we need to have money in order to achieve anything in life, we also need to be free of money and to hold money lightly. A friend of mine once said, 'Some people hold their dollar notes so tight, the queen starts choking!' It's often said that 'money is the root of all evil'. This is a misquote. The correct line is: 'The *love* of money is the root of all evil.' You can have no money and yet still love it. Conversely, you can have money and not love it.

It is amazing to me how many people blame money (or their lack of it) for their problems. Don't blame or praise money. Money has never broken up a marriage. Money is neither good nor bad; it is neither moral nor immoral. It's your attitude towards money and your use of it, not the money itself, that determines the effect it has on your life.

Money only magnifies what you already are

Some people think of money as being like a pool. The water in a pool is stagnant. There is no inlet and no outlet. For these people, money must not be spent. For money to grow, it has to circulate; it must be spread around and it must be spent. People save for a rainy day and, sure enough, that is just what they get — a rainy day. How often do we hear people saying things like, 'If I could just win the lottery, or if I could just get a lucky break, then I would support a charity or do some other good with my money'? This is misguided thinking. In actual fact, the person who does not use their money for good when they have small amounts would not be generous with it if they found themselves with large amounts. Money can't make you what you're not; money only magnifies what you already are. Money does not make the man or the woman, it merely magnifies what he or she already *is*.

Money can't make you what you're not — money only magnifies what you already are.

Some people have said, 'If I won a million dollars, I would give it all away.' That would be foolish. If you won or made a million dollars and you invested it wisely, then over your lifetime you could give away well over a million dollars from the interest alone. Margaret Thatcher made this statement about prosperity: 'No one would remember the Good Samaritan if he'd only had good intentions; he had money as well.'

Poverty and welfare do not encourage an entrepreneurial spirit. Poverty and welfare keep people controlled, broke, contained, dependent, discouraged and locked in a cycle that can continue from generation to generation. The welfare mentality is about giving people handouts, but what people need are hand-*ups*. Like the Chinese proverb says: give a man a fish and you feed him a meal; teach a man to fish and you feed him for a lifetime.

Money has no mystical powers that can turn people into corrupt capitalists or virtuous paupers. It is what is in the heart of a person that makes their money either good or bad. Money takes on the characteristics of the person who has it. The only power that money has is the power you give it. In a gambler's hands, it will be squandered. In a drug addict's hand, it will be used to support bad habits. But in a prosperous person's hand, it will be spread about and invested wisely. Money is like electricity — it can be used to either warm something up or to burn something down. In and of itself, money is neither good nor bad.

Be a problem solver

One of the greatest lessons I ever learned is that the key to wealth, prosperity and making money is to solve problems.

...The key to wealth, prosperity and making money is to solve problems.

Anyone who has ever created wealth has been in the problem-solving business. People such as Bill Gates and the late Henry Ford made their money by solving problems. Bill Gates solves information technology problems and Henry Ford solved transportation problems.

A good friend of mine once said to me, 'Never complain about your troubles, Pat. They are responsible for more than half of your income.' That is exactly right! I am in the business of solving problems. Therefore, when I solve problems, I see money as a stream in my life — money comes in and money goes out. I see it as a stream when I invest in the education of others — I put time and money in and it comes back. Norman MacEwan, air vice marshall in the RAF, said this: 'Happiness is not so much in having as sharing. We make a living by what we get, but we make a life by what we give.'

The story is told of a midly successful young business-person who received a brand new Ferrari for his birthday. He drove his Ferrari into one of the roughest sections of town and parked it there.

On the curb was a six-year-old boy who looked at this man dressed in his pinstripe suit, seated in his red Ferrari and he said, 'Sir, you must be so rich!'

The man replied, 'I'm actually not that rich, but I'm doing okay.'

'But you must be rich!' insisted the young boy. The businessman looked down at the excited, dream-filled young boy and said, 'In actual fact, I've just turned 30 and my brother gave me this car as a birthday present.'

The boy's eyes grew bigger and wider and he said, 'I wish … I wish … I wish I could be a brother like that!'

The power lies with the giver, not the receiver

Your response to that story tells me what kind of person you want to be. You see, the prosperous, millionaire, abundance mentality understands that you've got to be able to spread your prosperity, not horde it. You've got to be the giver, rather than the receiver, because the power lies in the giving. If you don't understand that, you won't be successful.

What a mindset this little boy had! He didn't wish to be the one receiving that Ferrari, but the one giving it. That is the essence of prosperity. His goal wasn't to receive, but to give. He understood that the reward lies with the giver, not the receiver; the hero was the giver, not the receiver. So many of us are only worried about what we can get. We're so concerned with how many houses we can acquire, how many cars we can buy and how many watches we can own, rather than what's inside us. The power does not lie in what you own and acquire — and that will come to you one day — the power lies in what's inside you, because that's what will help you acquire the houses, cars and watches. Pity the person who is always the taker and not the giver.

Steps to prosperity

There are a number of steps to prosperity.

- *In life, you've got to be an earner.* You've got to earn an income. You've got to earn money. You've got to earn respect.

- *But to be an earner, you've also got to be a giver.* You've got to give something away. It's the timeless law of seed time and harvest that transcends every culture and age.

- Once you are a giver, *you progress to becoming an investor,* because the seeds you sow through your giving you can now invest.

- *And then, lastly, you become a harvester.* Most people stop at earning and so they never progress to being a giver, then an investor and, finally, a harvester.

That's why so many people never receive. You see, money has to flow, and it needs people to make it flow by giving money away. Money is useless in a stagnant pool. It needs to be a river.

Some people are content to have just enough money to get by. I've heard some people say, 'I just need enough money to put food on my table.'

When you think about it, that is a selfish attitude. We need enough money to put food on our table *and* someone else's. Why be content with having just enough money to look after your own limited circle of influence?

People with a millionaire mindset understand that you have to progress from earner to giver to investor to harvester. However, this does not work in reverse! You can't harvest before you sow the seeds. Life just doesn't work that way.

If I asked you, 'Do you want to prosper?' you would undoubtedly answer, 'Yes, I do!' But if we began to dig deeper into your subconscious, we may get a different answer. We know that this is the correct answer, but do we really believe it? The answer is in what some people call the heart, others call the soul and others still call the mind. It's that part of you that contains your belief systems. Perhaps you may find yourself asking, *Can I really be prosperous? Is it really possible?* You may find yourself thinking, *If only I lived in a better suburb*, or *Maybe I don't deserve prosperity*. If you have these kinds of thoughts, then you are sabotaging yourself through your subconscious.

> Money is useless in a stagnant pool. It needs to be a river.

You live through your subconscious

Did you know that you and I really live at the level of our subconscious? Let me illustrate: when you first learn to drive a manual car, it's difficult to balance the clutch with the gears. Sometimes your car will kangaroo jump, other times it will stall. But when you become comfortable with a manual car, your subconscious takes over and it becomes easy to drive. So you and I have got to get our mind to believe things through our subconscious.

Money, money, money ...

This leads me to another common issue with money: greed. Some people hold on to things very tightly — especially money. Money captures the minds of people because it is a necessary commodity in our lives. Bestselling novelist Paul Erdman once stated, 'The entire essence of America is the hope to first make money — then make money with money — then make lots of money with lots of money.'

Isn't it amazing how our attitudes surrounding money can change according to the situation? Some people see money as a curse. Others see money as the reason behind their predicaments. For some people, all they see is money.

Some people make excuses about money; that having a lot of it will taint them. Some people think they are too virtuous to have a lot of money. Other people feel a need to apologise for their wealth and wellbeing. But it is not wrong to be wealthy and prosperous. There is no shame in that. Money is not an evil thing — in fact, it is a good thing. What matters is what we *do* with the money that comes into our world.

> It is what is in the heart of a person that renders that person's money either good or bad.

When money comes to me, it becomes *my* money. That means it becomes submitted to *my* ethics, *my* philosophy and *my* values.

We need to get rid of the 'pie mentality' — the notion that there is only a certain amount of money to go around. Can you imagine if we applied that concept to every area of life? The truth is that there is an abundance of all things in this world — enough for all of us to have abundance. But if we have a 'stagnant pool' mentality about money, we actually clog the flow of prosperity. Be generous with your money, be a giver, be a sharer and watch what happens — you'll find it will come back to you. If you see money as a stream, rather than a pool, and allow it to flow out from you, then there will always be more flowing back into you.

Challenge:
See money as a positive tool

Do you have negative ideas and attitudes about money? Does the topic of money make you feel uncomfortable? If you want to develop a millionaire mindset, you need to be relaxed about money and see it for what it really is—a wonderful servant in the hands of a master who knows how to control it and to use it to make the world a better place.

Money is not the root of all evil. To paraphrase George Bernard Shaw, the lack of money is a major reason for all kinds of evil in the world today. If you ever want to develop a millionaire mindset, train yourself to think positively about money.

Chapter 9

Make failure your teacher

Where your focus is today, your future is tomorrow. Don't emphasise your past failures and regrets unless you intend to live there. Your mistakes are an *event*; they are not a permanent condition. Everything you need for your future is in embryonic form in your hand today. What do you have in your hand right now?

It is a tragedy when people whinge about what they don't have or what has been taken from them; when people lament their losses, rather than celebrate what they have. People mourn the loss of innocence at a young age, a lost relationship, lost money, lost houses or lost businesses. You can't do a thing about what has been taken from you, but you can do something about whatever it is that you have in your hand right now.

I was once in Canberra at a speaking engagement with over 1700 young people when a goth girl came up to me. She was wearing black from head to foot, her face was painted white and she just looked generally weird. She spoke with a gravelly voice: 'Can I talk to you?' I have to admit that she freaked me right out! She showed me her arms and I was horrified—they were cut and slashed all over.

It turned out that this girl, Victoria, had been sexually abused between the ages of seven and 17. She was a mess, but she had a dream. Victoria became involved in our drug and alcohol rehabilitation organisation and went on to help over 70 girls graduate from our program. Today she is a successful businesswoman. What changed? She had a dream and she got past her past.

What do you have now?

Business owners complain about not having the staff they would *like* to have, rather than focusing on improving the staff they *do* have. People complain about not having enough money and talk about what they would be able to do if they had more, rather than doing something constructive with whatever they have right now. It's not what has been taken from you that counts, it's what you do with what you have *left*.

Many years ago, one of my closest friends, an honourable man of great integrity, suffered a great injustice through bad information that had been given to him by an accounting firm. It caused him incredible hardship and left him bankrupt. As the disaster unfolded, I watched his business partners become bitter, disgruntled men. Yet my friend continued to stand tall. He went to his creditors and told them he would pay them everything they were owed, but his partners refused to be involved in any repayment to the creditors. It has been amazing to watch this man resurrect his finances out of the ashes.

How did he do it? He took the little he had left and invested it in knowledge and a new business venture. He realised that what was taken from him didn't matter as much as what he did with what he had left. Today he is one of the largest franchise owners in Australia and he recently took over the worldwide rights of his ever-expanding business.

Zig Ziglar once said, 'Optimists are people who, when they wear out their shoes, just figure they are back on their feet.' Robert Schuller talks about the distinction between an optimist and a pessimist using the 'glass half full/glass half empty' analogy. The optimist pours water into the glass, while the pessimist pours water out of the glass; one looks at what he can put in, the other at what has been taken out. If all you look at is what has been taken out instead of at what is in the glass, then that becomes a dominant mindset in your life and prosperity will not flow.

> It's not what has been taken from you that counts, it's what you do with what you have *left*.

The millionaire mindset makes failure a teacher

The person who refuses to prosper and who constantly looks at what is taken from him makes failure his undertaker. But the millionaire mindset makes failure a *teacher*. Which will you be? Consider the story about a young man who was involved in an oil venture. He eventually ran out of money and sold his interests to his partners. After a lot of time, energy and effort, they finally had a breakthrough and hit a gusher. The company is known today as CITGO. Then the young man who had left the business became involved in the clothing business, which turned out worse than his oil venture.

It seemed as though a lot had been taken from him. Certainly he had lost a lot — in fact, the man was flat broke.

He had a lot to complain about. Yet rather than be discouraged by what he had lost, he found his niche in politics and, over the years, historians have had many wonderful things to say about the great US president Harry S Truman. This two-time failure kept his focus on what he had in him that he could use, not on what had been taken from him. Truman became the 33rd president of the United States — not by virtue of what was taken from him, but through what he did with what was left over.

> Make plans to succeed, not to wallow in your loss.

Adversity causes some people to break — and others to break records. Take, for example, the great American athlete, Jesse Owens, who showed Adolf Hitler that perhaps Aryans were not the superior race with his incredible ability on the athletics track. It was discovered that the reason for his success was an incredible sickness that caused him to run faster. Then there's Lance Armstrong, who fought testicular cancer and went on to win the grueling Tour de France seven times — and is trying for number eight next year!

Lack of persistence leads to failure

Anyone who wants to prosper must work on what they have now. Those who are condemned to failure are those who complain about what they have lost, what could have been, might have been or should have been. Such complaining is pointless; it drains energy and is a prosperity thief. If a person's mentality throws up excuses that they were not brought up correctly or that they would have been a lot better off if only they'd inherited at least a small amount of wealth to build on, then that person is deceiving themself.

Eighty per cent of America's millionaires are first generation rich. Two-thirds of them are self-employed; they did not inherit opportunity, they created it from what they had. Napoleon Hill, author of *Think and Grow Rich*, once said, 'The majority of men meet with failure because of their lack of persistence in creating new plans to take the place of those which fail.'

When you have lost something, stop dwelling on it—leverage it to springboard you into a better future. Make plans to succeed, not to wallow in your loss.

'But I'm dysfunctional,' you may say. Others may say, 'I've had my heart broken!' or 'I've had a breakdown!' Welcome to the human race; everybody has baggage. Everyone has made mistakes. Everyone has been hurt or treated badly at one time or another. If you've messed up or if someone has messed you up at any time in your life, then you are the perfect candidate for success.

Get over it ... please!

You've got to get over your past. People are so concerned about their past failures—about slipping down a rung or two on the ladder of life—that they just don't try. If Humpty Dumpty knew he was an egg, perhaps he would never have climbed the wall. My advice to you is to climb it anyway! Have a go! Climb to another level! And if you slip, just keep climbing.

Here is some shocking news: nobody comes from a functional home. Everybody has some kind of dysfunction in their background. We are all, in one way or another, victims of dysfunction, but past mistakes, hurts, fears and failures should be the springboard to your future success.

You will learn more from the tragedies of your past than you will ever learn from the good times. You have to get over your past, become bigger than it and not dwell in any disappointment. Your prosperity quotient has to be greater than your disappointment quotient.

Many people get stuck in the past because they are continually looking in the rear-view mirror of their life. You cannot go forward if you are constantly looking backwards.

It's like the elephant at the circus. This beast is held captive by a small rope and a little stake in the ground, because when the elephant was a baby, the trainers tied a tiny rope around its ankle and attached the other end to a stake in the ground to keep it from roaming. The elephant never forgets that the stake and the rope prevent it from moving away. Even though it could easily break free, the adult elephant remains a prisoner of its past. What's your stake in the ground? What's in your past that is holding you captive?

Past adversity is often the window of opportunity

Winston Churchill made this great observation: 'Kites rise highest against the wind, not with it.' Past adversity is often the window of opportunity for change and betterment. The mind is a filter that enables us to see things. Life is not as it happens; life is how you perceive it. Many people don't prosper because they hold onto perceptions that were formed in the past. Other people are able to use the past for their advancement in spite of tragedy or pain from childhood, business dealings or relationships. The difference is perception. Some people bury the past and move on, other people keep resurrecting a corpse. A painful past makes a great building material for incredible towers of prosperity.

The late Reverend Ross W Marrs once said that if you took away his ability to fail, he would not know the meaning of success. He went on to say to let him be immune to rejection and heartbreak and he could not know the glory of living. Think about that! If you take away the ability to fail, the ability to feel rejection, if you inoculate yourself against heartache and heartbreak, then how are you ever going to become a bigger person?

A few years ago, a friend of mine decided to climb Mount Everest without an oxygen tank. This is what he said to me afterwards: 'Pat, the higher I went up that mountain, the less weight I could carry in my knapsack. I got to a point where I went through my knapsack and found my toothbrush and cut the handle off it because all I needed was the head of the toothbrush — I didn't need the excess baggage.' He said, 'There are some things you just cannot take with you to the top.' Don't be comfortable with old problems, commit to new solutions and prosperity.

> A painful past makes a great building material for incredible towers of prosperity.

It's not only our negative past experiences that can hold us back. There are two kinds of memories in life: good and bad, and both kinds of memory ruin prosperity. I love this quote from Walt Disney: 'I do not like to repeat success, I like to go on to other things.' What a brilliant statement! Bad memories are like chains around our ankles that hinder us from moving forward, whereas good memories can become hammocks in which we rest.

Challenge:
Get over your past and move on

What's in your past that may be holding you captive? You've got to leave the past behind. Only then can you create a future. There are some things you just can't take with you on your journey towards success.

To see prosperity in every area of your life, use your past as building blocks for your advancement. Bury the past and move on.

Chapter 10

Know what you want

What do you really want in life? I recently put this question to a group of real estate professionals. These people were high-income earners. Their response was that it's a very hard question to answer. I disagree. I know what I want in life — and if I can figure it out, so can you. I want to prosper. I want to create wealth. I want to help other people become wealthy. I want to help people who are disadvantaged go to another level. To do these things, I need money.

You must know what you really want to achieve in life before you can become prosperous. If you don't know where you are going, how will you get there? And how will you know when you have arrived? People often think that they know what they want, but when you ask them to articulate this they realise that they can't. People often simply say 'I want to be rich,' or 'I want to be successful,' but this isn't specific enough. Let's look at discovering what you really want out of life and how to get it.

'Do you want change or do you want dollars?'

I was in America once speaking at a large network marketing conference and during a break in sessions I went to get a coffee. (Whenever I'm away, I always go looking for a good espresso!) I was on my way to the coffee shop when a rather large gentleman came up to me and asked me if I had any change. I said to him, 'Do you want change or do you want dollars?'

He looked at me, surprised, and said, 'Are you kidding?'

'No, I'm not,' I said. 'I want to know what you really want.'

'I want to get some food,' he replied. 'I figure if you've got some change I can get myself a sandwich,' he explained.

I said, 'I'll tell you what, how about I buy you your whole meal?'

This idea appealed to him. 'All right, man!' he said, 'You from Australia? I always wanted to go to Australia.' (Now there's a millionaire mindset: he couldn't afford a meal, but he dreamed of flying to Australia!)

So I took the man to a deli and bought him a whole heap of food. Then I gave him $10. He thanked me and we went our separate ways.

The next day, I was in the lobby of my hotel when another man came into the lobby and approached me. 'You got some change?' he asked me.

So I said, 'Do you want change or do you want dollars?'

'I want to get some food,' he said.

'Great!' I replied. 'Let me take you down to the deli and I'll buy you a meal.' (I knew where the deli was, by then!)

He said, 'No, no! Just give me the money!'

Now, I was born at night, but not *last* night, so I said, 'No, no, no! If you want food, I'll buy you food.'

'I just need some change, man!' he replied.

Again, I asked him, 'Do you want change or do you want dollars?'

'I just want some money,' he said, getting frustrated. Then he walked away.

I watched him as he walked out of the hotel lobby and approached a lady outside who happened to be one of the conference delegates. He asked her for some change and she offered him some food — a sandwich and some fruit that she had just bought. Incredibly, he refused it, saying, 'No, I don't want it!'

> You need to know exactly what you want in life and be able to articulate it...

Funny, isn't it, how you can think you want something, but when it's offered to you, you knock it back because you really don't know what you want. What do you really want? So often we don't know the answer to this simple yet fundamental question.

Many of us declare, 'I don't know what I want, but I know what I *don't* want.' This won't get you anywhere. You need to know exactly what you want in life and be able to articulate it, then base your life decisions on that knowledge.

A young man who knew what he wanted

Some years ago I was in California, and I was asked to visit a young man who was about 19 years of age and dying of AIDS. As I approached the hospital ward I could hear the sound of something gasping for breath. It sounded more animal than human. As I got closer, I discovered that the sound was coming from the young man I was about to visit. AIDS had completely ravaged his body.

When I walked into his room, what was meant to be a 19-year-old man looked like a 95-year-old man. His hair had fallen out and he had lesions down one side of his face. One of his eyes was shut tight and his face was black and blue. He was having difficulty breathing and, once the nurse helped him to sit up, we were introduced. Then I asked him, 'Steve, how are you doing?'

> If you can define what you want, it will be a lot easier to obtain.

In a sad, husky voice he replied, 'Not good.'

I asked him if the medication was helping. 'No, it's not helping me,' he said. Then he looked at me and said, 'A minister came in here yesterday and prayed for us all to get healed.'

'Steve, did anybody get healed?' I asked. You see, I believe in miracles. I've seen some miracles in my time. *You* may not believe in miracles, but you *are* a miracle!

Through his one open eye and with a look of sadness, anger and confusion, he said, 'No, man. Nobody got healed.'

I then blurted out the dumbest question I have ever asked in my 47 years on this planet: 'Steve, don't you want to be healed?' What a dumb question to ask a 19-year-old guy whose life had been savaged, ravaged and eaten away by this hideous disease!

I'll never forget what happened next. He turned to me, one side of his face looking battered and bruised, one eye shut tight, lesions down one side of his face. On the other side of his face his skin was clear and healthy. Tears fell down his cheek. 'No, sir,' he said. 'I don't want to be healed. I just want to be loved!'

At least Steve knew what he wanted. The question is: do you? I made sure that for the remaining few weeks of his life Steve was surrounded by friends and members of our community. I made sure he was embraced by the love he so desperately craved.

What a tragedy that most people go through life and cannot articulate in a sentence what they really desire. As the proverb says, 'He who is everywhere is nowhere.' What do you really, really, really want? Can you define it? Can you specify what it is? Or is it some pipedream or something you read in a magazine or saw in a movie? If you can define what you want, it will be a lot easier to obtain.

Rocky, Rocky, Rocky...

In their book, *The One Minute Millionaire*, Mark Victor Hansen and Robert Allen relate the story of Sylvester Stallone's struggle to get his first major film role:

> *In 1974 Sylvester Stallone was a broke, discouraged actor and screenwriter. While attending a boxing match, he became inspired by a 'nobody' boxer who 'went the distance' with the great Mohammed Ali.*
>
> *He rushed home and in a three-day burst of creative output produced the first draft of the screenplay entitled* Rocky.
>
> *Down to his last $106, Stallone submitted his screenplay to his agent. A studio offered $20000 with either Ryan O'Neal or Burt Reynolds playing the lead character. Stallone was excited by the offer, but wanted to play the lead himself. He offered to act for free. He was told, 'That's not the way it works in Hollywood.' Stallone turned down the offer, though he desperately needed the money.*

Then they offered him $80 000 on the condition that he wouldn't play the lead. He turned them down again.

They told him that Robert Redford was interested, in which case they'd pay him $200 000. He turned them down once more.

They upped their offer to $300 000 for his script. He told them that he didn't want to go through his whole life wondering 'what if?'

They offered him $330 000. He told them he'd rather not see the movie made if he couldn't play the lead.

They finally agreed to let him play the lead. He was paid $20 000 for the script plus $340 per week minimum actor's scale. After expenses, agent fees, and taxes, he netted about $6000 instead of $330 000. In 1976 Stallone was nominated for an Academy Award as Best Actor. The movie Rocky *won three Oscars: Best Picture, Best Director and Best Film Editing. The* Rocky *series has since grossed almost $1 billion, making Sylvester Stallone an international movie star!*

Nothing will happen until you decide to prosper

Stallone knew what he wanted and was seemingly prepared to make any sacrifice in order to get it. If you want to prosper, you have to focus on what you want. You have to make a choice; you have to make a decision. Nothing happens in life until you make a decision. Your decision could be anything. Try:

I'm going to commit to becoming prosperous!

I'm going to commit to creating wealth!

I'm going to commit to building a great business!

I'm going to commit to building a house!

I'm going to commit to having a family!

What do you want? You've got to choose. The singer Gloria Estefan once sang about sealing our fates with the choices we make. What choices have you made about the kind of life you want to have? If you don't know what you want, how will you recognise what you want when you see it? If you're single and you want to be married, have you chosen what kind of spouse you want?

> Sometimes we just haven't taken the time to think through what it is we actually want.

I once had a client who wanted to get married. One day I asked her, 'What kind of man do you want?'

She replied, 'Oh, anyone will do. At my age you can't be too choosy.'

We were sitting in a cafe and I pointed to a rather large and dishevelled character seated at another table. 'What about that guy over there? The toothless, hairy one,' I suggested.

'Oh, no!' she quickly replied, 'I wouldn't want someone like him.'

'Okay,' I said. 'That's one sort ruled out. So, what kind of man do you want?'

If you're married, let me ask you this: what kind of marriage do you want? Every marriage has its own culture, its own personality (some have the personality of a war zone!). What kind of personality do you want your marriage to have? Every bank account has its own personality, too. Businesses are the same. Is the personality of your business one of wanting to grow, to increase, to prosper, to invest, to gain knowledge and to learn? Apply this question to every important area in your world: what kind of business, career, marriage, family, home, lifestyle … do you want?

Sometimes we just haven't taken the time to think through what it is we actually want. We think we kind of know what we want, but we struggle to articulate it. This is a very basic starting point for developing a millionaire mindset. It's really not a difficult question — it's not rocket science. Life is so simple, you have to go to university to mess it up!

What do you want in life? You have to choose. What car do you want to drive? Where do you want to live? Don't go straight to 'I can't afford it'.

Sylvester Stallone couldn't afford to turn down a $20 000 offer for his script (let alone $330 000!). Making up your mind is the first thing. The rest is about time, decision-making, planning, input and growth. But if you don't know clearly what you want, how will you ever get there?

If you aim for nothing, you're bound to hit it!

Apple co-founder Steve Jobs convinced one-time PepsiCo CEO John Scully to take the helm of Apple by asking him, 'Do you want to spend the rest of your life selling sugared water, or do you want a chance to change the world?' Jobs forced Scully to take stock of his present situation and to think about what he really wanted from life.

Don't settle for a 'sugared water existence' when, in your heart of hearts, what you really want is to change the world. Remember, if it's a mist in your mind, it's a fog in your world. If you aim for nothing, then you're bound to hit it!

Financial problems or mind problems?

About a year ago I was doing some consulting for a large real estate firm. They asked me if I would do a mentorship program with some of their top sales agents and I grasped at the opportunity because I figured it would present an opportunity for me to learn from them as well.

I met with one of their agents who, as soon as I walked into the room, I could tell had some real issues. I immediately assumed he was a heavy smoker because of the stench coming from his body. And I also assumed he had an alcohol problem — again because of the telling odour. What I did not know was that this man had a financial nightmare on his hands. To my surprise, as we began to talk I concluded after about 30 minutes that this guy earned a huge income. As a matter of fact, he was earning half a million dollars in net income each year. Yet, he looked at me and said, 'I have a financial problem.'

...if you don't know clearly what you want, how will you ever get there?

I soon discovered that this gentleman had a $35 000-a-month gambling habit. He also had an incredible alcohol problem. As well as that, he was a prolific user of cocaine. This guy did not have a financial problem, he had a discipline problem and he could not see it. He couldn't see that his problem wasn't money, it was that he couldn't discipline his addiction. So often you and I assume we have a financial problem, when in reality we may instead have a vision problem, or we may have a priority problem, or we may have a spending problem — we buy things we don't need and we can't afford because we want to impress other people.

You've got to ask yourself: what is the real reason I lack things in life? Sometimes the problem you think you have is not the real issue and a problem well defined is a problem almost solved. If you can't define the real challenges that are hindering your prosperity, you'll never prosper. It could be a mindset. It could be your upbringing. It could be that the culture you were brought up in told you money is evil. This is a mind virus that you must offload.

What does your world look like?

I used to run programs to help rehabilitate drug addicts and we had an 86 per cent success rate. The theme of our program was 'turning nightmares into dreams'. We graduated around 400 young men from heroin addictions, cocaine addictions, ice addictions and so on.

After they graduated, I would ask them, 'What will your world look like when you leave here? What will your future look like when you get out of this program?'

They would reply, 'Well, I'm free of drugs, I'm happy, I'm getting on with my mum and dad, and my mum's hugging me…' These boys had to define what they wanted before they could leave the program. Once you decide what you want, the choices you make to get you there are much more simple.

You and I would surely agree that if those boys couldn't see their future, rest assured that their drug dealers could!

I remember one day a lady came into our facility and I asked her if I could help her.

She said, 'I've come to pick up my dream.'

It didn't immediately occur to me what she meant, so I said, 'You're here to pick up your dream?' (I thought that perhaps she was interested in me!)

'Yes,' she said. 'My son, Robbie. He came in here nine months ago and he was a nightmare. Now he has graduated, he has become a dream. Where is he? Where's my dream? Where's my boy?' Such beautiful, positive, uplifting words!

What's your problem?

The only thing we really had to do with some of those guys was to get them to think differently. There are plenty of detox centres in my city with a low, 14 per cent success rate. The truth is, we don't have a drug problem, we have a vision problem. Young people with hope and a future do not inject drugs into their veins.

I am of the opinion that a clear vision of your future will inspire you to put up with any pain in the present. Ask any Olympian who has won a gold medal and they'll agree. The joy of the gold medal causes all the pain of past training to fade away into insignificance. A mother giving birth to a child will put up with nine months of weight, struggle and morning sickness. And when that child is born, the overwhelming joy pushes all the pain of pregnancy and birth into the past.

> ...A clear vision of your future will inspire you to put up with any pain in the present.

I believe most people get so busy and stressed wondering how their plans are going to happen rather than simply focusing on the purpose for their plans and believing that they actually will happen. You see, if you have a reason, you'll find a way.

So often in life people don't find a reason—they are so gunshy due to past hurts that they can't see any way that their plans will come to fruition. So the first port of call for a prosperous mindset is to clearly define your *why*—your purpose and your dream.

Adults sometimes tell young people, 'Don't expect much out of life' or 'Your father was an alcoholic, so what would you expect?' or 'The apple doesn't fall far from the tree.' This kind of mindset displays nothing but lies that rob people of their future. I can assure you that I fell a long way from my family tree—I was catapaulted out of it—but it didn't stop me from realising my dreams.

> If you haven't decided what you want, then there is no point having a plan.

I said at the beginning of this book that I want to help make people rich. And one of the steps towards that goal was to start a club, which I have now done. My dream is that through this club I will be able to help 10 000 people become millionaires, or at least to help them start thinking like millionaires. You, too, can become a part of this club. (See the back of this book for more details.)

A road to nowhere

If you haven't decided what you want, then there is no point having a plan. People often start planning before they've figured out what they want, but it doesn't work that way.

'I'm planning for my future,' someone may say.

I always ask what your future looks like. If you don't know, then how can you plan for it? If you're planning to play a game of football, but you don't know where the game is being played, how can you possibly turn up to play? If you don't know where the goalposts are, how can you score?

Challenge:
Make up your mind — what do you want?

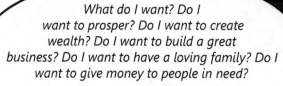

What do I want? Do I want to prosper? Do I want to create wealth? Do I want to build a great business? Do I want to have a loving family? Do I want to give money to people in need?

It's amazing how many people can't answer these questions. Can you?

Close your eyes and paint a picture in your mind of what you'd like your life to look like. What's your family like? What is your career like? What is your world like? How would you think? How would you feel? How would you speak? How would you live?

You need to know what you *really* want. Everybody ends up somewhere, whether they mean to or not. Don't wonder how you got to the end of your life. When you know what you want, then you can make a plan to get it.

Chapter 11

Pay attention

My mother was a wonderful woman. As a child, I remember that as I would go out to play with my friends, my mother would call after me...in my Italian name, 'Pasquale, pay attention when you cross the road. If you get hit by a truck, don't you come crying to me! Pay attention!'

I also remember how one of my teachers, Mrs Bird, would come up behind me in class while I was busy daydreaming and she would slam her hand down on my desk and shout, 'Pat Mesiti, pay attention!' My mother and Mrs Bird both understood a powerful principle in developing a millionaire mindset: the principle of focus.

Sometimes when I travel I get back cramps. One day I was in Singapore and a salesman was selling an electronic massaging pad that you wear on your body. 'This is very good for massage,' he informed me. 'But only use it for 10 minutes a day — very dangerous.' He pulled out a photo of Bruce Lee. 'Bruce Lee used this machine to build muscle,' he said.

I was sold! 'Give me two,' I said.

On the plane back to Sydney, I thought to myself, *I have a seven-hour flight from Singapore to Sydney. I can look like Bruce Lee by the time I get off the plane.* So I went into the lavatory and placed the electronic pads on my stomach under my shirt. I was travelling with one of my daughters and we'd been upgraded. So there I was, sitting next to my unsuspecting daughter with a glass of champagne in my hand.

There were three levels of intensity on the massage machine: low, medium and high. Those who know me know that I am not a low intensity kind of person. And to me, 'medium' is another word for average—something I never want to be! So I went straight to the high setting. I pushed the power button...

All of a sudden I was screaming in agony—needless to say my daughter was mortified. Her only comment was, 'I'm *so* not here!'

I learned a very important lesson on that flight. You see, I wanted the Bruce Lee six-pack without having to focus on getting it. Now I'm into down-sizing—instead of the six-pack, I've chosen a one-pack! I've learned that reaching your goal involves focus, as well as time and sustained effort; there are no shortcuts to lasting prosperity.

Get focused

Focus is a discipline and, as such, it needs to be developed. To have a millionaire mindset, you need to learn how to keep your mind focused on what you want. Your mind is like a muscle. Just as regular exercise and physical exertion build and strengthen our muscles, the mind is strengthened by focus. For muscles to grow, they must be exercised and fed. You have to focus on them in order for their ability to increase. If you want to see increased wealth or progress in any area of your life, you must keep your focus on what you want and not allow distractions to rule you. Whatever you feed will grow, and whatever you starve will die. Successful people keep their focus firmly and clearly on their desired goal.

Successful people keep their focus firmly and clearly on their desired goal.

Once you've figured out exactly what you want, the next challenge is to stay focused on it. It is impossible to achieve what you want if your attention is constantly being spread all over the place. Focus requires a specific goal. You need to stay with your main game. Focus gives you an edge, because the longer you work at something, the better you get at it.

Focus is made up of a number of factors:

F — Forward planning
O — Overcoming distractions
C — Committing to a plan
U — Understanding your objectives
S — Sustaining effort.

- *Forward planning.* Know exactly what you want in life and plan how you are going to get it. Have long- and medium-term plans, but also have a plan for today. If you don't plan your day, your day will have a mind of its own. Think about what needs to be done today to keep you on track. Then stick to your plan.

- *Overcoming distractions.* Anything that draws your attention away from what you are trying to achieve is a distraction. Life is full of them. What are the things that easily distract you? Be aware of these and understand your propensity to be distracted. What is it that typically distracts you at the most important time?

Be alert and, wherever possible, remove the source of distraction.

- *Committing to a plan.* Keep yourself accountable. Make a to-do list and prioritise everything on it. Someone once said they often feel like a mosquito at a nudist colony — so much to do, but they don't know where to start! There is always a lot to do. Prioritise what you need to do, devise a plan and commit to it.

- *Understanding your objectives.* As well as knowing *what* we want, we need to know *why* we want it. In my own life, it's not just a matter of knowing that I want to be prosperous, it's also about knowing why I want to be prosperous. Know the answer to the questions 'Why am I here?' and 'What am I here to do?' Have clearly defined objectives.

- *Sustaining effort.* Nothing worthwhile comes without significant effort. Anything worth having is worth working towards. As a well known advertisement says, it won't happen overnight, but it *will* happen. Don't give up. Don't get discouraged. Keep working at it — that's what leads to success.

Prosperity won't happen in a day, but it will happen daily

When I was running my drug rehabilitation centre, many young men would come into our program and say, 'I want to get off drugs, man!'

I would respond by saying, 'Fantastic! Once you have qualified to enter our program, we will look after you, feed you, clothe you, pay for your medical expenses, get your teeth fixed, educate you, teach you a trade so that when you graduate you can enter into a business opportunity and create a future for yourself. We'll make sure you have a mentor who works alongside you. We'll make sure you get the most outstanding counsellor we can find.

'However, here's the catch: for nine months your life belongs to me. You will get up at six every morning. At 7 am, your bed will be made, your teeth will be brushed and you will have shaved and showered and be dressed ready for the day. You will have breakfast at 7 am — not 7.07 am! After that you will wash and dry the dishes. You will learn how to work as a team.

Don't give up... Keep working at it — that's what leads to success.

'At 9 am you will enter into some therapy. You will learn about yourself, why you do what you do. At 10.30 am, you will have morning tea. After that you will go back to class. At noon you will sit down for lunch. After lunch, you will learn a trade or a skill for four or five hours. When you come back, you will give us a urine sample — just to make sure that you have kept yourself clean. You will have someone stand and watch you provide that sample because we don't want you swapping it with someone else's.

'After that you will go for a work-out. You will then sit down for dinner — on time, showered and ready to enjoy a good meal and some fellowship. You will then make a phone call to your mother, father or anyone you have lied to, ripped off, used or abused and you will make restitution as best as you can. The lights go out at 9.30 pm. You will go to bed at 9.30 pm sharp — not 9.40 or even 9.35. You will be up the next morning at 6 am, ready to face the new day.

'This is your life for nine months.'

On hearing that schedule, some young guys would think, *I don't want to get off drugs* that *badly!* Here is the problem: those young men did not want to focus. They wanted an instant fix.

People often come up to me at the end of a meeting as I am getting into my car, looking forward to some personal time after pouring my heart out, and they say, 'Pat, can I have a minute of your time?' Then they unload years of problems and want me to solve them immediately. They don't want to focus; they just want a quick fix. Prosperity does not come in an instant, it comes daily. What you do *daily* determines what you are *permanently*. Prosperity doesn't happen in a day, but it can happen daily — and it requires your focus.

Stay focused

For real and lasting change to happen in your life, you have to be prepared to stay focused on your goal. If you want to be prosperous, you have to stay focused on the things that will lead you into prosperity. It's amazing how many people change their perspective or lose their desire because their focus wanders. Ultimately, your life will head in the direction of your focus. People don't really decide their future; they decide their focuses and habits. What they focus on and their habits will decide their future.

A few years ago I was building my dream home and I took it upon myself to be the master gardener. My father was an outstanding gardener — he could grow anything. So I planted some flowers and trees. But after some time, I noticed they weren't growing.

One day I was with a group of friends and I lamented that the soil around my house wasn't as fertile as the soil at my father's house when I was growing up. One of my friends said to me, 'I don't understand it, Pat. I live near you and the plants in my garden are flourishing. Have you watered the plants?'

I suddenly realised that I hadn't watered my plants. I had wanted them to grow by themselves, but had forgotten that for plants to flourish, they need sunlight — which my garden had; they need the right soil — which my garden had; and they needed water — which my garden did *not* have! I had not focused on my garden. I had wanted results, I had wanted the fruit, but I had not focused on the fundamentals required for a flourishing garden.

You also need to focus on what you already have that will help you along the path towards your goal. I had the soil and the sunlight the plants needed — I was so close to a flourishing garden. I just needed to focus on remembering to water the poor things!

Focus can be incredibly powerful. It can help you overcome seemingly insurmountable obstacles and bring about change in the face of what might seem like overwhelming adversity. I was once talking to a woman who had been through seven marriages (she was obviously very good at it!). I asked her, 'What is the one thing those seven marriages had in common?'

> Ultimately, your life will head in the direction of your focus.

Her answer was very telling. 'Men!' she said. 'Abusive men.'

I knew there was something else going on here, so I asked her to tell me her history. It turned out that she had been brought up by an abusive and alcoholic father. Then when she grew up, she met a guy who had a few challenges, but she thought she'd sort him out once she married him. So she ended up marrying an abusive, alcoholic wife-beater. She eventually got divorced and then married one of his friends. (What is it they say about 'birds of a feather'?)

Over the following years, every one of her husbands was an abusive man. After hearing her story, I asked her this question: 'When are you going to stop trying to rescue

Daddy?' She was focused on her past experience with her father and her life was following the direction of her focus. Be aware of the origins of your wrong thinking.

Whatever you focus on will progress

Focus on what's right, not on what's wrong. Whatever you focus on will progress and whatever you neglect will regress. Many people get sick because they neglect their bodies through smoking, poor eating habits, lack of exercise or sleep. But a change of focus can turn around years of neglect. If someone in poor physical condition decides to focus on becoming healthy, then change will happen. As they give up smoking, start eating well, begin exercising regularly and generally begin to live a wholesome lifestyle, their physical condition begins to improve. Why? Because you get what you focus on.

So often we create an environment of neglect around ourselves. Consider for a moment the room you are in right now. I'm assuming that your room is in a reasonable state of order, cleanliness and repair. But if you were simply to leave the room right now and not come back into it for a number of years, do you think that room would be in the same condition on your return? Of course not. There will be dust and cobwebs everywhere, the furniture and curtains will have faded, the paint may have started flaking here and there, and there will probably be some evidence of vermin around the room. The room's condition will have deteriorated simply through neglect.

It's the same with our lives. If we neglect some part of our world, then that area will regress. So many people fail to focus on what they want and do nothing to get it. Later, they wonder why they always seem to be going backwards in life.

Learn to value results

We live in a results-oriented culture. People will generally judge you or accept you on the basis of one thing: results. Prosperity is about results. If I didn't know how to prosper and get results, I wouldn't be in a position to write this book. I have learnt to value results. I want results.

Some people say, 'I just want to be happy.' But what does happiness mean? Where's the tangible result in that? Others will say, 'I want peace.' What does peace mean? You and I need to define what we want so that there is a measurable result attached to it. Otherwise, how will we know when we've achieved our goals?

Distraction is the number one enemy of focus.

What was that? I wasn't paying attention ...

We need to destroy the mind viruses that are crippling us. One of the most prevalent mental afflictions is called 'distraction.' Distraction is the number one enemy of focus. There are so many things out there vying for your attention, but most of them are nothing more than distractions that will take your focus off the things you should be paying attention to.

Thomas Fuller, chaperone of Charles II of England, once observed, 'He that is everywhere is nowhere.' In order to achieve anything, you need to focus on a target. Distractions put distance between you and your goal. They interrupt your progress. They cause you to stray from the path that is taking you to your goal. They encourage your mind to wander. They lead you into forming — or reverting to — bad habits that will hold you back. They cause you to expend your energy non-productively. They make you time poor. Above all, they destroy your focus.

…And I want it yesterday

Another enemy of focus is the 'I want results and I want them now' mindset. Almost 99.9 per cent of the time, that's not how things work. Focus involves time, effort, energy and input. It requires a single-minded approach.

If you desire financial growth, business growth, success growth, wealth growth or relational growth, but you are not prepared to put in the necessary time and effort to develop your mind muscle through sustained focus on your desired goals, then you will hinder your progress towards prosperity.

The environment surrounding your mind will determine your success

In order to prosper, you need to create an environment in which you can focus. It's your responsibility to create the environment you desire—whether for your business, your home or your relationships.

Removing or learning to ignore distractions is part of this process, but you also need to put practices and principles in place that will develop an environment around you conducive to staying focused and to sharpening your mind.

Your mind is your greatest asset, so give it some attention and get it under control. Most people's income shrinks to the level of their mindset. Focus on putting some stuff in your mind that will enlarge your mindset.

Feed your mind with the kind of material that will help keep you focused. How many books do you read each month? How much motivational or educational material do you listen to? Do you have success mentors helping you to create an environment for wealth creation around your mind? In what ways are you developing and strengthening your mind? When wealth and prosperity come your way, will you know what to do? Focus on creating an environment around you that encourages and promotes the pursuit of success and prosperity.

You'll never possess what you are not willing to pursue

You will never possess something that you are not willing to pursue. Focus requires clarity and specificity. You need to pursue not just some abstract ideal, but something tangible—a specific amount of investments, a certain type of relationship, a certain position or opportunity. Think about the kind of people you want in your world; which specific individuals would you like to build an association with? Pursue relationships with people who are ahead of you, more skilled than you, more intelligent than you and more creative than you. Being around people like that will help lift you to another level.

When wealth and prosperity come your way, will you know what to do?

Prosperity has to be actively pursued. That's what focus is all about—relentless pursuit. Here are a few general things you must focus on pursuing in order to become more prosperous:

* Excellence

* Integrity

* The wellbeing of others

* Positive acquaintances

* Knowledge.

Another important principle in developing focus is to pay attention to your attitudes. One particular trap to watch out for is the trap of complacency. Many people who have reached a certain level of success make the mistake of becoming familiar or comfortable with their level of success. They say familiarity breeds contempt, but in this context, familiarity breeds regression and failure.

Focus means sticking with something to its completion.

Familiarity can manifest itself in a number of ways — as arrogance, as overconfidence, as a loss of passion, as a lack of care or as presumption. Great sportspeople or teams are often beaten by relatively lowly ranked opposition because of familiarity.

Focus also requires an understanding of the 'big picture'. While it's important to stay focused on the details and the small things that may seem insignificant, ultimately, nobody is motivated by details. The big picture keeps us motivated.

In my book, *Attitudes and Altitudes*, I speak about the difference between 'whats' and 'whys'. The *whats* are the tasks you have to do to pursue prosperity: the calls you need to make, the people you need to meet, the books you need to read, the deals you need to close, and so on. Often the whats are seen as menial or mundane.

That's why the *whys* are so important — they are all about your vision. They are what drives and motivates you and keep you focused on the big picture. You need to have a grand vision that provides a broad context for every decision, every choice and every strategy along the way. Your vision also provides a framework for learning and for your relationships.

Look at the big picture, but don't ignore the details

Focus is all about maintaining an awareness of the big picture, while simultaneously keeping an eye on the details. Alvin Toffler put it this way: 'You have got to think about "big things" while you are doing the small things, so that all the small things go in the right direction.'

In his book, *Thinking for a Change*, Dr John C Maxwell makes some great points about unleashing the potential of focused thinking. He identifies the following benefits of maintaining focus:

- Focus harnesses energy towards a desired goal.

- Focus gives ideas time to develop.

- Focus brings clarity to the target.

- Focus will take you to the next level.

Focus means sticking with something to its completion. Harry A Overstreet once stated, 'The immature mind hops from one thing to the other; the mature mind seeks to follow through.' It requires discipline and concentration.

In his book *Focus: The future of your company depends on it*, Al Ries offers a great illustration of the difference between focus and lack of focus. He describes how the sun is a powerful source of energy, sending billions of kilowatts of energy to the Earth. Yet with a hat and some sunscreen, you can bathe in the light of the sun for hours with few ill effects.

A laser, on the other hand, is a weak source of energy. A laser takes a few watts of energy and focuses them into a single stream of light that can drill into a diamond or erase a cancer. That's the power of focus. Unleash the power of focused thinking and you will reap the results.

Here are seven key areas of focus that I believe are important for anyone aspiring to become prosperous:

- Focus on *yourself*.

- Focus on *your communication skills* — including your posture, your facial expressions, your tact and diplomacy and your attitude.

- Focus on your *area of expertise* — become an expert at what you do best.

- Focus on *knowing people* — your client base, for example. Know what motivates them. Know their dreams and desires and what they want from life.

- Focus on your *strengths* — maximise your effectiveness. A few years ago, the USA and China faced off in the world table tennis championships and China won easily. When they interviewed the coach of the Chinese team afterwards, they asked him how it was that his team was able to beat their opposition so convincingly. He said the difference was in what the two teams focused on. He observed that the Americans' approach was to find someone with a good backhand and train him to try and have a good forehand, whereas the Chinese approach was to take a player with a good backhand and match him up with someone who had a good forehand so they could work off each other's strengths. In other words, they focused on their strengths, not their weaknesses.

- Focus on *follow-through* — one of the greatest keys to success is following up with clients and following through with what you said you would do.

- Focus on *developing momentum* — momentum creates and builds energy for future success.

- Focus on *being persuasive* — people are persuaded when you show them how **they** will be advantaged, not how *you* will be advantaged. To create wealth and prosperity, you must learn the art of positive persuasion. This requires focus.

Developing a millionaire mindset requires a focused mind. Spend some time each day forcing yourself to focus your mind on the things that matter in your world.

Challenge:
To prosper, pay attention to what you want

Start focusing now if you want prosperity in your life. Discipline your mind. Recognise distractions when they come your way and resist them. Realise that your mind is your greatest asset and give it some attention. Feed it with great books and positive audio tapes. Whenever you are in your car, listen to successful people teach you principles and attitudes of success. If you want a higher income, a better marriage or a larger business, then you have to learn to think a certain way. Make a decision today to start focusing!

To develop a millionaire mindset, you need to stay focused on creating wealth, prosperity, on your business or on creating the right kind of thinking about yourself and your world.

Chapter 12

Growth happens by choice

Many people try to achieve success by making cosmetic changes, but the reality is that only inner improvements will lead to outer ones. Only with real changes to our mindsets and attitudes will real results be seen. At the end of the last chapter, the top of the list of things you needed to focus on was yourself. What do I mean by this? Well, you need to focus on your own personal growth and development. This will help you to prepare for maximum effectiveness. Abraham Lincoln once said, 'If I had eight hours to chop down a tree, I'd spend six hours sharpening the axe.' You need to sharpen your mind first in order to see effective success in business, career and relationships.

To have a true millionaire mindset, you must be big on the inside, and you must grow even more; you must have new experiences and learn and change through them. But true growth must come from within — you must seek it and truly want it for yourself. No matter who you are or what you are doing, there's always room to grow. You have got to understand that you have to break through ceilings in order to grow. The same level of thinking that got you to where you are now won't get you to where you need to go. In this chapter we are going to look at what growth means and how it affects your mindset, and also examine some strategies that will help you grow in order to attain greater prosperity.

How big are you on the inside?

A beautiful little girl was walking down a street. She was wearing a white dress, pink shoes and pink ribbons flowed from her hair. The little girl was eating a huge ball of fairy floss. A gentleman knelt beside the little girl and asked, 'Sweetheart, how can such a little girl like you eat such a big ball of fairy floss?'

She looked straight back at the man and said, 'Sir, I'm a lot bigger on the inside!'

How big are *you* on the inside? And are you growing? You see, there is always room to grow—one man's ceiling is another man's floor. For example, many would agree that world motorcycle racing champion Valentino Rossi is a prosperous person. But when you compare him to businessman Donald Trump, there is a big difference. Then compare Donal Trump to Bill Gates, and you will see another big difference. In other words, one person's limits are just another person's foundation.

What do you have to offer?

You need to pay attention to your growth and make sure there's always something in your tank to keep you going. This applies to a whole range of things, whether it is money or something less tangible, such as experience. If you're running on empty, you'll find yourself siphoning up gunk from the bottom of your tank. But if you're full, you are always able to give something back. In order to give something away, you need to have a surplus. For example, how can I teach other people about how to become successful and prosperous if I don't have a wealth of personal experience in these areas? Someone might say to me, 'I want to be a motivational speaker like you.'

My reply would be, 'Well, what have you achieved to provide a background of experience from which you can impart to others?'

To have anything to give, there has to be something of value within us. Regardless of religious beliefs, I'm sure everyone would have to agree that one of the most powerful speakers on the planet is Dr Billy Graham. He is an amazing communicator who is able to gather enormous crowds and hold people's attention with his authority. When Dr Graham speaks, people listen. Some new upstart preacher could get up and give the same message as Dr Graham, and yet he wouldn't attract the same attendance or the same attention. Why do people come in droves to listen to Dr Graham? Because he has a wealth of experience; his speeches carry the weight of his experience.

> Without struggle, we don't gain strength. Without pain, we don't progress.

This kind of experience only comes our way through constant exposure to challenges. Without challenge, we don't grow. Without struggle, we don't gain strength. Without pain, we don't progress.

Growth is a process, not an event

If you want progress in your life, you've got to pay attention to your growth. You see, growth is a process, not an event. 'Yes, but I went to one seminar years ago and it changed my life,' someone may say. There is always going to be much more to it than that. A seminar might give you a kick-start, but it's how you proceed from there that really makes the difference. People will sometimes come up to me and ask, 'What's the one book I need to read?' Again, one book or one CD can be enough to get you started, but change is an ongoing process.

Prosperity is a process. Some people win the lottery and all the money is gone within a few years. Why? Because their wealth was the result of an event, not a process; they never learned how to be prosperous. They never developed a millionaire mindset. They suddenly found they had a lot of money, but there was no process of growth to learn how to handle their new wealth. We all need to grow — in our relationships, in our beliefs, in what we know, in knowing what we are capable of doing and in our understanding of ourselves. (It has taken me 45 years to just start to understand myself — I still haven't got it totally figured out!)

Prosperity comes by choice, not by chance.

Growth mostly happens by choice, not by coercion

Generally speaking bribes and threats — carrots and sticks — do not motivate us to grow. Growth mostly happens by choice, not by coercion. Prosperity comes by choice, not by chance. Fear, threats and bribes might motivate you for a while, but they won't have long-term effects. Growth requires focus. It is determined by what you surround yourself with and what you feed into your mental, spiritual and emotional bank account. Merely desiring growth is not enough; there has to be change. Growth equals change and change equals growth.

Many people don't grow in life. These people always have the same problems. For them, nothing ever changes or progresses. A man once came up to me and said, 'Pat Mesiti, I'm sick of all your happy claptrap.' He continued, 'I've had 20 years of experience. What could you know that I don't?'

His wife was standing behind him, looking embarrassed.

I said to him, 'Sir, you haven't had 20 years' experience, you've had one experience over and over for 20 years. And as a result you're miserable, you're tight and you're poor.'

His wife was standing behind him cheering me on! You see, he had never grown. He just kept doing the same thing year in and year out and nothing ever changed. His life was like a treadmill — he was walking through life, but he wasn't going anywhere. Some people never graduate from the kindergarten of life. Their wealth never grows because their mindsets stay small and limited.

Try a millionaire mindset on for size

Here's an example of something very practical you can do to help your personal growth, to help develop your millionaire mindset: the next time you go out to a restaurant for dinner, go to one that's just a bit nicer than the kind of restaurant you would normally eat at. And when you go to that nice restaurant, don't look at the menu and say to your companion, 'You should get the chicken. It's the cheapest thing on the menu.'

I recently came home from a trip and my wife, Andrea, picked me up from the airport. I told her to book any restaurant she liked for dinner that night. Needless to say, it turned out to be expensive, but it was a great night!

When you buy your wife flowers and there is a choice between a $15 bunch of roses that looks okay and a

$40 bunch that looks beautiful, don't think to yourself, *Well, she won't know that I bought her the cheaper bunch.* She may not know it, but you will!

Every now and then you should try on a millionaire mind-set for size. Go on — I dare you! You never know, you might find it fits better than you think!

Growth has nothing to do with your age, it's all about your desire for success. Age does not determine your growth, input does. Build your life in increments. When you've worked out what you want, start moving your life towards it. One change will pave the way for the next, creating the opportunity for you to grow.

Your growth is determined by a number of factors. Here are three things that I believe will help you grow in order to attain greater prosperity:

- *Emotional implantation.* You need someone in your life who will encourage you and help you to see what you can't — and who is far enough away to see what can be done.

- *Repetition.* Develop habits that lead to growth.

- *Discomfort.* This is the real determining factor. Discomfort will cause you to grow. For your muscles to grow, they must experience a level of discomfort through exercise. You will learn more in adversity than you will when things are going well. It is what you believe and how you act in your worst moments that will determine who you really are.

You're only responsible for your own prosperity

It's important to understand that you are responsible for your own growth and development, but not anyone else's.

Sometimes we can think the changes that need to happen in our world depend on changes in the people around us. I'm sure you can think of a few people you would love to change!

You may have heard the story of the man who came home drunk night after night, causing his wife all kinds of grief and disruption. Finally this wonderful, patient woman had had enough. In her frustration, she decided to do something about it. She went to a costume shop and hired a red devil suit and a pitchfork. She decided she would try to scare him into changing his drunken ways.

One change will pave the way for the next, creating the opportunity for you to grow.

When he arrived home late that night, drunk as usual, she jumped out in front of him screaming and holding the pitchfork in front of him. Her husband merely glanced at her and said, 'You don't scare me — I married your sister!'

Pay attention to your growth

Become pregnant with growth, because eventually you will give birth to new things. Here are 10 'As' of personal growth — 10 straightforward and simple strategies that can help you move beyond average growth into exponential growth, wealth creation and prosperity.

1. *Analyse.* Growth starts by analysing exactly where you are right now. Analyse your current situation. Are you in a place of contentment or are you hungry for something more? If you go to a doctor and she analyses your problem incorrectly, you won't be able to treat it effectively. It's the same when it comes to personal growth.

2. *Aim.* Set your sights on where you want to be. Most people run their lives on the principle of 'ready, fire,

aim.' To move ahead, you need to aim correctly before you shoot. Many people shoot at anything — they have no specific target. Instead of taking aim, they randomly fire away, putting bullet holes in walls. Then they take a crayon and draw a target around one of the bullet holes and call it a bullseye. That is not a bullseye; it's a whole lot of bull!

3. *Adjust.* Be ready to make adjustments as you go. If you find you are not heading in the direction you want to be headed — or if you are not experiencing the kind of growth you were hoping for — then you must change direction now. There's a story about a large battleship that was ploughing through heavy seas with low visibility when it received an urgent message: 'Adjust your course. You are heading for a collision.'

The captain of the ship sent a stern reply: 'I know exactly where I am heading. Adjust your course!'

The voice came back over the radio, 'Adjust your course. Danger is imminent!'

The captain grabbed the microphone: 'If you want to avoid a collision, adjust your course! I am a battleship!'

Back came one final cool reply: 'If you want to avoid a collision, adjust your course. I am a lighthouse!'

If you are heading in a direction that is not leading you into growth, be flexible, learn how to swallow your pride and adjust your course!

4. *Align.* Align yourself with the right people. Align yourself with people who will stretch you and who can teach you; people who will challenge your thinking, your mindset and your motivation. Align yourself with people who will change your perception

of things and who have already been where you want to go. If you are earning $100 000 a year, hang around people earning a million dollars a year. If you are a millionaire, hang around with billionaires.

5. *Affirm.* Affirmation is important to growth. Affirm your dream. Affirm your core beliefs. Affirm yourself. Affirm others.

6. *Anticipate.* Anticipate growth. Anticipate productivity. Remember, your mind and your wealth will go in the direction of your focus. Your life will follow your focus. If you anticipate opportunity, prosperity and growth, then that's what you'll get.

7. *Apply.* Apply truths and apply what you really believe. Apply what you know. I recall the story of a French tightrope walker named Blondin who, to the amazement of a large crowd gathered at the top of Niagara Falls, succeeded in walking a tightrope suspended across the huge thundering waterfall. On his way back across the falls, the people clapped and cheered, 'Blondin! Blondin! Blondin!'

If you anticipate opportunity, prosperity and growth, then that's what you'll get.

He asked the crowd if they believed he could do it again. They cheered louder and they clapped harder. Then he asked if anyone was prepared to sit in a wheelbarrow and let him wheel them across the rope. The crowd fell silent.

Everyone believed, but nobody wanted to apply their belief! You need to apply and practise what you believe to achieve personal growth.

8. *Adopt.* Adopt the right habits. They will help you grow into the person you want to be.

9. *Abandon.* Abandon bad habits, abandon negativity, abandon bad relationships and abandon old mindsets so that you can replace the old with the new.

10. *Accelerate.* Put your foot down and accelerate your growth. Growth occurs in forward motion. To grow, we have to accelerate and move forward. Accelerate beyond difficulties, excuses, what the market is telling you towards your future growth.

Invest in personal development — you're worth it!

In life you will be remembered for two things: the problems you solve and the problems you create. One of the laws that governs our growth and prosperity is that you and I must be committed to being a problem-solver. There are far too many problem-creators around! I'm sure you have had some experiences with these types of people. There are far too few problem-solvers in this world. Problem-solvers always increase in value, while the value of problem-creators is always decreasing. That's why problem-solvers become prosperous people. You and I will be rewarded for the problems we solve and we will be remembered for the problems we create.

I often get the opportunity to speak to real estate groups and I thoroughly enjoy the vibe, the fun and the excitement of these hard-working people who work in one of the most noble of professions in the world: sales!

Recently, during a break in my speaking sessions at a conference in Australia, I walked into a restaurant and began speaking to a waitress. She asked me what I did, so I told her I was a speaker and that I was speaking at a real estate conference.

She said, 'Oh! Oh! You're just the person I need to see! My real estate agency is doing a lousy job! They have had my house on the market for three months and they haven't sold it yet. I'm about to re-negotiate with them because I don't want to pay them any commission.'

I looked at this young lady in bewilderment. 'How much do you get paid by the hour?' I asked.

'I get paid $11 an hour,' she told me.

'Do you know why you get paid $11 an hour?'

'Because I'm a waitress,' she answered.

'No,' I said. 'That's not why you get paid $11 an hour. If I answer the question, promise me you won't hit me.'

'Why would I hit you?' she asked.

'Because you haven't heard my answer yet.'

'I promise I won't hit you,' she said, 'I'm intrigued.'

So I told her, 'You get paid $11 an hour because that's what you are worth.'

There was dead silence. I continued, 'That's the worth you bring to the marketplace. I'm not talking about your worth as a wonderful person or as a mum or as a wife, I'm talking about your value to the marketplace.'

I went on to say, 'Now, I'm familiar with the real estate agency looking after your house. It has about 150 years of sales experience. On top of that, it has one of the most prestigious brands in the country. They also have television advertising. And they have an incredible database, a huge list of wonderful clients who they have served for 20 to 25 years in one location. To be honest, you really ought to increase their commission and give them an incentive to sell your house. They get paid according to the problems they solve. Is your house an important part of your life?'

'It's my most valuable asset,' she answered.

'Then you must reward them for the problem they are solving for you. You don't want an agent who is worth $11 an hour.'

Add value to yourself

As I said earlier, in life you will be remembered for the problems you solve and the problems you create. A cleaner is paid a different hourly rate to a barrister. Why is that? They both get paid for the various problems they solve.

So understand that you've got to add value to yourself in life. If you want to add value to yourself, then solve problems and create futures for people. If you are the kind of person who does that, then you'll add value to yourself as well as to those you help.

I have met people who undercut themselves too much — they don't charge enough for the work they do and for the problems they solve. If you add value to people, they will consider that the money they pay you is irrelevant. *One of the laws of life is that in the absence of any value we will always argue about the cost.* If you clearly add value, then people won't have a problem paying you more money.

If you educate yourself to become a prosperous person, then you will add value to yourself. Education is not expensive — ignorance is! Ignorance always costs. Contrary to popular opinion, ignorance is not bliss; ignorance is pain and it can lead to a lack of prosperity.

Become a problem-solver by educating your mind in the field in which you want to prosper. Go and study your craft for 10 to 15 minutes a day and become the best you can be at it. Add value to yourself and people won't worry about the fees you charge them.

If you will grow a bigger you, you will grow a bigger world — and you will grow a bigger income. It all starts with shifting your mind. It all starts with personal development.

Just as your body can't function on a steady diet of junk food, neither can your mind feed itself on a diet of TV shows, tabloid newspapers and gossip magazines. If you will commit to feeding your mind, you will grow your value to others around you.

...you will be remembered for the problems you solve and the problems you create.

As Benjamin Franklin once said, 'Empty the coins in your purse into your mind and your mind will fill your purse with coins.' No wonder so many people are broke! It's because they don't feed their minds.

If you change your mind, the rest will follow.

Education is not expensive — ignorance is!

So, how does change happen? It comes through education and the commitment to personal development. Remember, it's called *personal development* for a reason. I was recently working out at the gym with my personal trainer, who is so buff he belongs on the cover of *Men's Health* magazine. I said to him, 'I can't wait for the day when you do all the work, Jason, and I get the body!'

He said, 'That'll never happen!'

'I know,' I admitted, 'but it's a good thought!'

Most people want the results of prosperity without the commitment to making it happen. I often ask people: if you paid someone $100 000 a year to run your business the way you are running it now, would you fire them? Most people answer, 'Yes!' So, nine times out of 10, I tell them that that's why they're not prospering. You see, I wouldn't fire me, because I know that I am my best asset.

Why? Because I have committed to work on my mind so I can build a prosperous mindset.

Become more, then you'll have more

Your mind will either build you a prison or a palace, and that is determined by the materials you use. Which do you want to reside in—a prison or a palace? A prison locks you inside. A prison contains you. A prison allows you no freedom. In a prison, you run around taking orders. In a palace, on the other hand, you are given free reign. In a palace, people recognise your worth. In a palace, you can do so much for people in need. Which is the healthier of the two options?

You must be committed to your personal development. All of us can have more. How? By *becoming* more. You can become more than you are right now by focusing on your personal development. Jim Rohn once wisely said, 'Success is not to be pursued; it is to be attracted by the person you become.' The person with a prosperous mindset, a millionaire mindset and an abundant mentality does habitually what broke people do rarely—they commit themselves to their own prosperity.

A little while ago I was listening to an outstanding speaker at a conference. I was frantically taking notes, totally captivated by this man's wisdom and insight and the angle from which he explained business principles. He was able to say so much with so few words.

I realised he had a resource table at the back of the room, so I quickly turned to one of my young assistants and said, 'Quick! Here's my credit card. Run to the speaker's resource table before the end-of-session rush and buy everything on the table.'

One of the keys to prosperity is this: learn to follow instructions. Never promote anybody who can't follow instructions. This young man was about to learn a lesson in following instructions. He rushed away and I went back to my frantic note-taking as the speaker continued. The young man suddenly returned and said, 'Pat, have you seen how much stuff is out there?'

Now, I had not told him to go out and count the available materials. My instructions to him were to buy everything on the table. So I told him to go back and do exactly that.

> You must be committed to your personal development. All of us can have more.

A few minutes later he came back and said, 'Pat, sorry to interrupt you, but I have calculated how much everything on that table will cost. There is about $7500 worth of material there.'

Again, I had not asked him to be my accountant, nor had I asked him to do an inventory and provide me with a bill of cost. So once more I said, 'Please, go and buy everything on that table before the rush!' I continued my note-taking, absorbing everything this incredible, prosperous speaker was saying.

The young man returned again and quietly said to me, 'Pat, I just want to ask you a question.' In a rather sombre tone he said, 'Is it worth it? It's going to cost you $7500!'

Your thoughts determine your priorities and your priorities should determine your spending habits. I looked him in the eyes and said, 'Young man, the clients I speak to are worth it. When I address people, they're worth it. And more importantly, my mind is worth it!'

The young man bought the material for me and I turned that investment of $7500 into half a million dollars. So, who got the better deal: me or that great speaker? I did, because I fed my mind and made a commitment to my personal development.

Your life prospers when your priorities change

Are you worth your investment in your personal development? Do you value yourself enough to feed your mind? People want better homes, better cars, better watches and better holidays without becoming better people. Money isn't the problem — commitment to personal development is the problem. Show me a person who is committed to their personal development and I will show you a person who will add value to themselves, to their clients and to their businesses. You see, your thoughts determine your priorities and your priorities should determine your spending habits.

...your future is sculpted by the chisel of choice.

The other day I was speaking at a convention being held at a casino and a young man rushed up to speak to me. 'Pat Mesiti, thank you for sharing with us today! Your message changed my life. I want to buy your books and CDs, but I can't afford it,' he said, as he puffed on a cigarette. 'My friend, who is a salesman, bought your materials. You really flicked his switch! He then went out and sold an $11 million deal. I'd love to get your materials too, but I can't afford it.'

Later that evening I was walking past the hotel's bar during happy hour. I caught sight of this same young man rushing towards the bar. I have never seen someone run so fast to happy hour in all my life! I watched him as he responded with excitement to the bar promotion of two drinks for the price of one — that's two drinks for $15. I saw him whip out his credit card and continue to buy more drinks. That young man had a very happy hour!

A couple of hours later, as I walked past the casino watching people wasting their money, I noticed the same young man frantically playing a slot machine. He had a cigarette packet and a tray of drinks beside him, hoping that luck and prosperity would come his way.

The next day this young man approached me again and said, 'Pat Mesiti, I loved your presentation this morning—even more than yesterday's. I'd love to buy your materials, but I just can't afford it.'

I said to him, 'You smoke, don't you?'

'Yes, I do,' he responded.

'How many packets do you smoke?' I asked.

'About one or two a day,' he said, 'depending on my stress levels.'

In Australia a packet of cigarettes costs about $10. So that's at least $3650 a year up in smoke for this young man. His drinking habit also would have been costing him $2000 to $3000 a year. Add to that his slot machine spending, which was probably another $1000 a year. That is a grand total of $7650 a year up in smoke!

I said to this young man, 'Son, you're wasting almost $8000 a year on smokes, alcohol and gambling. Yours is not an issue of affordability, yours is an issue of priorities. When you make a commitment to prioritise feeding your mind, then your world will begin to prosper.'

You see, your future is sculpted by the chisel of choice. And the choices you make are determined by the investments you have made. I have found that it's only when you are frustrated with your present condition that you'll begin

Growth happens by choice

to invest in creating a greater future. Until then, you will stay miserable. When the pain of your present frustration hits you hard enough, then you will begin to commit to investing in your prosperity.

I believe that the reason so many people do not prosper in the western world is that their lives are simply too comfortable. My wife and I are involved in supporting orphanages in developing countries. If you give a child in a developing country a $30 loan, they will turn that into an enterprise. And, incidentally, they will pay you back. That's inspiring!

When we give these children books and other reading material it's amazing how they respond. They are like children who have been given a delicious meal. They consume those books with such hunger! They are hungry to learn, hungry to win and hungry to prosper. They may live in a poor country, but they're not broke in their thinking. They have a prosperity consciousness.

If you will master your thoughts and make a commitment to personal development, if you will change your inner image, it will change your outward life. It is impossible to avoid the outward manifestation of your inner world.

Let me illustrate this further. A few years ago I was interviewing a young lady who was a well known model in Australia. Unbeknown to a lot of people, this young lady had a drug addiction. She said to me, 'Pat, I feel like a slug. As a matter of fact, I feel worse than that — I feel like the trail of slime that slugs leave behind. That's why I use crystal meth.'

It's amazing to consider that her outward manifestation was a reflection of her inner world. Her beauty wasn't enough; she was overcome by the ugliness of her inner feelings.

It is impossible to avoid the outward manifestation of your inner world.

Your inner world is the product of your personal development

Like this model, your own mindsets will determine your actions and your actions will define your character. Your character is not defined by your words, but by the quality of your deeds. In life there is nothing cheaper — or more expensive — than words. Words are powerful, but where do they come from? They come from your inner world, which is a product of your personal development.

When I was 18 years old, I made a goal that I would read material and feed my mind so that whenever I opened my mouth I would have something to say that would have an impact on my listeners. You see, if you want what you've never had, you must be committed to doing what you've never done before. People desire a change of lifestyle without a change of thinking. They want everything around them to be better — the cars, the house, the investments — but they themselves don't want to become better. Your growth is a process; it's not an event. It happens daily. What you do daily will determine what you are permanently.

My great friend Dr Robb Thompson said this: 'In life you will never possess what you are unwilling to pursue.' You'll never possess a prosperous or an abundant lifestyle if you are not committed to its pursuit. Your mind is a muscle. A muscle that is not exercised and fed will weaken and will stop growing. Sometimes that muscle needs to stretch and tear so that it can rebuild, expand and strengthen. You and I have mindsets that we need to stretch and tear. Why? So that we can grow stronger, healthier mindsets.

To have a prosperous mindset, you've got to do what prosperous people do. You've got to read what they read. You've got to go where they go. You've got to attend the events and seminars they attend. I've discovered that those who most need to grow and feed their minds are often the least likely to do so. What a tragedy that they are too lazy or too comfortable to grow!

Your environment will determine how you function

The prosperous mindset also recognises that you will function according to the environment with which you surround yourself. There is power in your environment. A few years ago I was conducting a program amongst children in one of the most destitute areas in North America. Over 80 per cent of the adults were unemployed, and over 80 per cent of the young people had a drug problem. It was one of the worst ghetto areas I have ever seen.

After we finished the program one night, I was back in an apartment with some friends and a few of the program team members when there was a knock on the door. I opened the door and found a gorgeous little girl standing there all alone. She looked up at me and said in a thick Southern accent, 'Ah missed ma bus!'

I later discovered that our bus driver had forgotten to tick this little girl's name on the bus list as she got onto the bus that morning. As a result, he hadn't looked for her when he departed that night. Perplexed and concerned, I looked at my watch and noticed that about two and a half hours had transpired since the bus driver had departed. I wondered what her mother must be thinking!

Something about her appearance caught my attention and I asked one of our female program members to take this young girl to a medical centre for a health check. Medical staff ran some tests and soon discovered that this girl was riddled with sexually transmitted diseases. We learned later that her mother had sold her for little vials of crack to sick men on street corners.

This little girl's name was Precious. I can guarantee that she never felt that way! I determined that we had to do whatever we could to get her out of that environment. You see, your life will function according to the environment around you. If you want a happy marriage, create the right environment around you. If you want happy children, you've got to create the right environment for them. If you create a dysfunctional environment, please don't expect a functional result. If you create a poverty mindset, don't expect a positive result.

...your life will function according to the environment around you.

Human beings are meant to prosper, not lack the essentials of life. Human beings were created to enjoy a life of abundance of health and possessions, not to suffer abuse and hunger.

We took Precious out of that environment. We provided a good education for her. We found her a new home with great foster parents who loved her and cared for her. Today she has graduated from medical school and is serving her community. She is no longer a victim of her environment — instead, she is creating a better environment for herself and for others who come into her world.

What kind of environment do you want? If you had never seen a motor vehicle before and I wanted to sell you one, I may tell you everything about it — the chassis, the cylinders and the engine capacity — but if I forget to tell you that your car will only function on roads, you will drive off not knowing some important facts about cars: they do not function in water or in the air! Cars are meant to function in one environment only — on roads. In the same way, the environment you create around you will determine how you function.

Everyone is influenced by their environment and by the people around them. Who is influencing you? You wouldn't let someone deliberately push you off course, but you may allow someone to gently nudge you off course in small increments. A boat can sink because of a small hole in the hull. It's the same with your mind. Allow positive influences from successful people to stretch and grow your mindset. If you want a prosperous mindset, you must be committed to the process of personal development and education to feed your mind, to feed others in your world and to add value to your worth.

> Allow positive influences from successful people to stretch and grow your mindset.

Prosperous people pursue mentors

Some people are committed to staying as they are. As a result, they get what they have always got. When it comes to our education, there are three types of people. First, there is the naive person who says, 'One person can teach me everything.' Second, there is the arrogant person who says, 'Nobody can teach me anything.' Then there is the prosperous person who says, 'Someone can teach me what I need to know in *this* area of my life.' A prosperous person who is committed to growth will pursue successful people as mentors. Sometimes they will not be able to access them physically, but they can usually access their teaching resources. In life you will learn from your mistakes or your mentors. Guess which of the two is easier to learn from?

To increase your life, focus on increasing *you*! Your focus on becoming the person you want to be will propel you towards your goal. Whatever captures your focus today will capture your future tomorrow. Your future prosperity lies within the confines of your mind. Everything you need is already in your mind in seed form. Like your garden, you need to nurture, prune and water your mindset. You grow a great garden by pruning off old branches, by fertilising the soil and by weeding and watering it regularly. Your mind is the same; it needs your regular attention.

Businesses and relationships don't stop growing—*you* do! If you stop growing, your business and relationships eventually will stop growing, too. The prosperous mindset habitually does what the broke mindset does rarely—it invests in personal development.

Challenge:
Commit yourself to acquiring knowledge

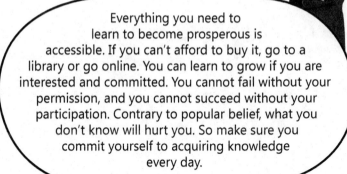

Everything you need to learn to become prosperous is accessible. If you can't afford to buy it, go to a library or go online. You can learn to grow if you are interested and committed. You cannot fail without your permission, and you cannot succeed without your participation. Contrary to popular belief, what you don't know will hurt you. So make sure you commit yourself to acquiring knowledge every day.

Chapter 13

How to make good decisions

How do you make decisions? Simple: you choose and you refuse. We choose the things that are good for us and we refuse the things that are not. When you get married, you choose the person you are marrying and you refuse all others. (If you know what's good for you!) You choose according to what you value and if you know what you value, your choices are easy.

Our decisions lead our lives. Our choices determine our destiny. Your decisions should come from your focus; decide what you want and focus on it. Then you continue to make decisions in keeping with your focus. Wrong decisions are a result of wrong input due to a lack of focus or a lack of clarity. Decision making is all about taking responsibility for the direction of our lives.

The opposite of this is blame — trying to shift responsibility for whatever is not happening onto someone or something else. People who look to blame others for the things that are wrong in their lives are actually undermining what they are trying to build. We all have a tendency to blame at times. The reality is, however, that blame is never an effective strategy for progress. You never feel better just because you've shifted responsibility through blame. Blame chips away at what is valuable. It actually results in dishonour and a fragmentation of what you are trying to build.

Choices are easy if you know what you value

A little while ago, I was sitting having dinner on my own in a hotel in Auckland. I'm no great stud (I'm more like a garden gnome on steroids), but as I was sitting there in my suit having dinner, a rather attractive woman came up to me. Now, I have dinner with people all the time, whether male or female. I'm not particularly paranoid about this as a rule, but there are exceptions. I feel comfortable with most people, but others give me a kind of vibe or an inner warning and this woman was in the latter camp. She asked me if I was staying in the hotel.

> Your decisions will either strengthen or weaken your focus.

'Yes, I am,' I said.

'Are you dining alone?'

'Yes, I am.'

'Can I join you for dinner?'

I changed my reply. 'No,' I said. 'I'm having dinner on my own, as you just asked me,' I politely explained.

She seemed somewhat taken aback at my refusal. 'Let me get this straight,' she said. 'You don't want me to have dinner with you?'

I said, 'There's nothing I'd like more than to have dinner with you. However, I've actually met you before.'

She was surprised. 'No, you haven't,' she said.

'Yes, I have,' I replied.

She started trying to place me, trying to remember where we may have met. 'Well, what do you do for a living?' she asked.

'I'm a speaker,' I replied.

'Did we meet at a conference you spoke at?' she asked.

I didn't answer her question directly. 'I even know your name.'

'You know my name? What's my name, then?' she asked.

'Trouble,' I replied.

She laughed appreciatively. 'That's very funny. So, can I have dinner with you?'

'No!'

Now, I could have had dinner with her and it wouldn't have been wrong, but it wouldn't have been appropriate. Why? Because the vibe she was giving me told me she would be trouble. I value my wife and my marriage. I made a decision based *not* on the circumstances of my immediate situation, but on the basis of values and priorities that I have predetermined and on which I maintain my focus.

We all make mistakes from time to time, but we need to make decisions that are based on what we value. Again, let me ask you: what do you value? Figure out what's important to you, stay focused on it and make your decisions accordingly.

Your decisions will either strengthen or weaken your focus. What you focus on will progress. Progress is a result of a concentrated effort in the right direction; it happens by choice, not by chance. We choose to keep moving ahead by making decisions. Neglect requires no effort, no energy and no decision. Actually, it does involve a decision: the decision *not* to make a decision.

Take charge of your life

Some years ago a young man in my drug rehabilitation centre stormed through my door. He was feeling very sorry for himself — he was having a pity party all by himself. He looked at me, frustrated, and said, 'Pat, I didn't ask to be born!'

You and I must decide to take charge of our lives.

I calmed him down and said, 'Brett, you are absolutely right. You didn't choose to be born, but you can choose how you live. Some of the troubles you have been through were not your fault, but how you respond is your choice and that will make all the difference in the world.'

There are some things in life you don't get to decide; your birthday, for example. Like Brett, you may say, 'I didn't ask to be born!' Generally speaking, we don't get to decide how or when we die either. But we have a lot of choice about what happens in between those two events. We *can* choose *how* we live.

Without a doubt, there are things that happen to us in life that are beyond the power of our decisions. Some people are abused or treated badly by their parents or other people in their lives. I've met young men whose lives have been totally devastated because their fathers committed suicide when they were young boys. Did these young guys choose that? No.

While we may not have any power of decision over how people hurt us, abuse us, desert us or let us down, we do have the power to choose to move on from these experiences and not allow them to rule our lives. These are the choices we need to make. A millionaire mindset is a mindset that decides that the circumstances of the past will not necessarily determine our future.

A poverty mindset thinks like this: 'Life just happens to me. This is my lot in life and I just have to live with it.'

A millionaire mindset thinks like this: 'Well, that may have been my lot in life, but I'm going to create a different world for myself.' You need to decide to create your future. The greatest ability you have as a human being is the ability to choose, to decide. You and I must decide to take charge of our lives.

Our choices determine our destiny

So how do you learn to make right decisions? For a start, you need to learn to value the right things. We must make decisions based on an understanding of what is of value. In the absence of an understanding of value, you will always argue cost. A kilogram of rocks and a kilogram of diamonds weigh the same. Of course, diamonds are much more valuable, but if you have no understanding of the relative value of rocks and diamonds, how would you know which to choose?

There is a direct relationship between what you value and how you spend your money. I was once in a bookstore with a friend buying a cookbook. I was at the sales desk paying for the book and it registered at $129.95. My friend couldn't believe the price.

'How could you spend $129.95 on a cookbook?' he asked me incredulously.

I looked at him and said, 'The guy who wrote this book has been a chef for 27 years. How much money do you think 27 years of experience is worth? Where else can you buy 27 years of experience for $129.95?'

As far as I was concerned, being able to buy the benefit of 27 years of cooking experience for only $129.95 was an absolute bargain! This particular book represented real value to me, so I was willing to pay the price asked in order to progress my own culinary ability. My friend saw no such value, so for him the book cost too much.

How you spend your money determines what you value.

Determine what is valuable and you'll make good decisions

How you spend your money determines what you value. If I value my time, I will spend money on things that will free up my time. If I value money, I will use my money to make more money. If I value my health, I will spend money on things like a gym membership and healthy food. If I value family, I will spend money on great holidays and other activities that create a happy family life. If I value my wife, I'll spend money on flowers, restaurants and gifts. As it says in the Bible, 'Where your treasure is, there your heart will be also.'

Once you determine what is valuable—what is a priority and what is irreplaceable in your life—you will make decisions accordingly. You'll even be prepared to take significant risks if it means pursuing something of value. In his book, *Locking Arms*, Stu Webber relates a great story that illustrates this point.

It's about two soldiers — Jim and Bill — who served together in the trenches during World War I and the deep friendship that developed between these two buddies serving together in the mud and the misery. Month after month, they were stuck in a stalemate, pinned down in the cold and the filth of the trenches, under constant fire.

Every now and then, one side or the other was commanded to rise out of the trenches and throw themselves into danger, only to crawl back to the trenches to bury their dead, lick their wounds and wait until they had to do it all over again.

In the midst of all this hopelessness and misery, Jim and Bill forged a strong bond, talking about their lives, their families and their hopes for the future.

On one of these fruitless charges, Jim fell, severely wounded, while Bill made it back to the relative safety of the trenches. Jim lay suffering in no-man's-land, alone beneath the night flares as the shelling continued. The danger was at its peak. Bill was determined to reach his friend to rescue him from his awful predicament, but the commanding officer refused to let Bill leave the trench. While his back was turned, however, Bill went over the top. Ignoring the horror around him, Bill made it to Jim and somehow managed to get him back to the safety of the trenches. But it was too late — by the time Bill got him back, his friend was dead.

One self-righteous officer, seeing Jim's body, cynically asked Bill if it had been worth the risk.

Bill did not hesitate: 'Yes, sir, it was,' he said. 'My friend's last words made it more than worth it. When I got to him, he looked up at me and said, "I knew you'd come."' Bill had made a decision based on what he valued, no matter what the risk.

Challenge:
Decide to be decisive

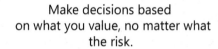

Make decisions based on what you value, no matter what the risk.

What are the things that you really value? Do your values drive your decision making? Do you have a clear sense of being in control of your life? Or do you let other people and circumstances make your decisions for you?

Having a millionaire mindset means being a decisive person. Take charge of your world today—decide to decide.

Chapter 14

Get some help!

To develop a millionaire mindset, you're going to need some help. (Presumably, you already know that, otherwise you wouldn't be reading this book!) You need role models in all areas of your life: career, business, character, family, wealth — in everything that matters. There's an ancient proverb that says, 'He who walks with the wise shall be wise.'

If you want to grow and prosper in life, then you need to pay attention to your associations. You need to connect yourself to people who've done what you want to do, who've forged paths to prosperity that you can follow. The company we keep can make or break us. As the saying goes, if you want to fly with the eagles, don't hang out with the turkeys.

The great Olympic pole vaulter, Bob Richards, once said, 'There is greatness all around you — welcome it! It is easy to be great when you get around great people.' My father used to say to me, 'Tell me who you walk with and I'll tell you who you'll become.' Who are you hanging around with? If you are hanging around with small-minded, negative, complaining people, then you'll become like them. If you hang around positive, big thinking, can-do people, you'll become like them.

You become like those with whom you associate

Many of the lessons I've learned about relationships have come out of the great relationships I've had. Dr Robb Thompson from Chicago has been a great mentor to me in this area. I've learned a few things about associations from him.

First, those who are closest to me will determine the outcome of my life. It's not *what* you know so much as *who* you know. The associations you embrace will determine both the consequences and the rewards of your life.

The second thing I've learned is that those who cannot increase you will eventually decrease you. You must be careful to choose people around you who will increase you. My friend who helped me buy a tie I wanted for an extra $100 added something to my life.

The third lesson about relationships is that whatever you make happen for others, others will make happen for you. In your associations and relationships, never make the pleasurable people of today pay for the painful people of yesterday. For example, if someone rips you off in a business deal, you may say, 'I'll never trust anybody ever again! I'll never invest with anybody again! People have always ripped me off!'

If an honest person then comes along and presents you with an investment opportunity or wants to share a business opportunity with you, you will most likely turn them down. If you are still living in the painful memory of the past, you will treat the pleasurable person of today with contempt. That is a recipe for a relationship disaster.

Ask yourself, *Who am I hanging around with?* Where have they got me going? What do they have me reading? What do they have me believing? What have they got me feeling? You see, our relationships are an important part of our life. That's why it is critical that you manage your relationships well.

...never care for other people's problems more than they do.

I love connecting people. Recently I was speaking to a friend of mine about someone I had just met. 'Bill, I'd like you to make some time for my friend, Brian,' I told him enthusiastically. 'He's in an outstanding man.'

'Pat, how do you know he's an outstanding man?' Bill asked me. 'You spent only 30 minutes with him over a brief lunch.'

'I know him by his associations,' I responded. I knew that a good man does not have bad associations.

One of the key factors in associations is that every relationship will either feed a strength or a weakness in you. If you hang around people who feed you a negative, poverty mentality, then run. You've got to spend time with people who feed your strengths. Hang around people who will build an empire in your mind.

In your associations, never care for other people's problems more than they do. Many times people come to us and want us to solve their problems and yet they don't really care about their problems themselves. What a tragedy that some people constantly rescue others to make themselves feel good, and yet they have totally wasted their time because the person they helped does not really care. If you want to build prosperity, work with people who care for their problems and issues and are willing to work with you.

In your own life, what you respect will move towards you and what you disrespect will move away from you. If you have a good relationship with money and respect it, it will move towards you. If you respect people with influence and honour, they will move towards you. If you disrespect them, whether it's your government or your employer, they will move away from you. Your association with them will determine the level of your prosperity.

Three kinds of relationships

Everybody needs three kinds of relationships:

1. People we look up to and follow—mentors, coaches and role models

2. Peers with whom we can share our lives and to whom we can talk about deep issues

3. People who are following us.

This is not about levels of superiority or inferiority; it's just a matter of different kinds of relationships and how they work. We need to get our philosophy of life from the first group, not the third group. You don't go to your kids for advice on how to raise them. The people you look up to are particularly important because they represent what you want to become and what you want to grow into. Many people don't have anyone in their lives like that.

I've been fortunate enough in my life to have had personal input from some of the great prosperity thinkers of our time—people such as Zig Ziglar, Robert Kiyosaki, Denis Waitley, Brian Tracy and Stephen Covey, to name a few. How would you like that? Then do what I do. Get them in your car. And if you like something they say, push the rewind button and listen to it again!

When Mike Tyson was taking his direction from his coach, Cus D'Amato, all was well with him. He became the world's youngest heavyweight boxing champion. Cus D'Amato did three key things for Mike Tyson: he helped him find a sense of belonging by taking him into his family, he helped him believe in himself and he helped him to become something extraordinary. But when his level 2 and level 3 associations (described above) began to dictate his lifestyle and thought patterns, things went downhill.

...what you respect will move towards you and what you disrespect will move away from you.

Who is influencing your thinking? Who are you allowing to speak into your world? Who's your coach? Who are your role models? Who are the people you are allowing to influence the way you think?

Get your advice from the right people

Understand that if a person doesn't receive your words, they really shouldn't qualify for your time. Perhaps you have chased others for words of wisdom, but if you don't listen to them and take their advice on board, why should you qualify for one of the most precious commodities they have — their time?

So many people get wrong advice from wrong people. You've got to watch the source of your advice. Some people offer advice when it has not been solicited. I rarely give people advice when they have not asked for it — if people ask me for my advice that indicates to me that they are somewhat interested in hearing what I have to say. I am also careful not to offer advice to people with whom I don't have a relationship. Again, if I have a relationship with them, then I have some confidence that they will heed my advice. However, if I have a relationship with you and you were to ask me for my advice, then you don't take it and things go belly-up for you, why should I continue giving you my advice?

Take advice only from those qualified to give it

I was asked by a company in the United Kingdom to speak to the entire sales force at their opening to launch their business in Australia. They had brought their team over to Australia as a part of their rewards program. I was delighted and accepted their offer. Fantastic! I thought. The Brits have a great sense of humour. I'll be in for a very, very interesting night! And I was!

> I believe anyone can develop a prosperity mindset.

The evening arrived and there were about 200 people in the room. But before I got up to speak, the man who owned the company came up to me, noticed I had a lot of books and CD teaching packs with me, and said, 'Gosh, all this material for sale … You must be making some money!'

He looked at me and said it in such a sarcastic way that I turned to him and said, 'You know what? That's exactly what your company needs! A broke speaker to address its sales team!' My point was this: a speaker teaches primarily from his knowledge and his own experience. Without experience, he can't teach others! I like to practise what I preach.

When I finished speaking that evening, a man walked up to me, looked at me in a rather condescending way, and said, 'May I offer you some advice?' He didn't give me an opportunity to answer, but went on to give me his advice:

'Your speaking style is not what we Brits are used to. I would suggest you tone it down when you next speak to us.'

Now, I understand that there are some people who don't like my speaking style. That's okay — they don't have to like it, because that's my style and I'm very comfortable with that. I then asked this gentleman, 'Have you ever spoken in public before?'

'No,' he answered. And yet he considered himself an expert in public speaking!

Next I asked him, 'Are you willing to enter into a long-term relationship with me to help me grow?'

'No,' he answered again. He simply wanted to offer me some constructive criticism and then walk away.

The third thing that concerned me was this: I never asked him for his advice. This man proceeded to constructively criticise me without me asking for his advice.

If you are going to enjoy a prosperous life, get your advice from the right people. If you are a mentor to other people, never offer advice that is unsolicited. The moral of the story is this: some people have a flourishing business, but they own a poverty mindset. The owner of this British company had a great business — he was earning $100 000 a month — but he had a poverty mindset.

Success is learned

I believe anyone can develop a prosperity mindset. People often ask me whether I think anyone is born a leader. My answer is, 'No, we're all born babies!'

Leadership is a learned art. Success is learned. Prosperity is learned. That's why we need teachers — people who stretch our thinking, encourage us and help us grow. One of my close personal friends, a man who has helped me greatly in my life, is an owner of one of the largest tea and coffee franchises in Australia. In times of difficulty in my life he would repeatedly say to me, 'Stand tall, Pat! Stand tall!'

His encouragement and support have been critical to me at times. This is the kind of person you want as a friend — someone who will encourage you to think bigger, who will challenge you to grow and who will believe in you.

There are always people you can learn from

Thomas J Stanley relates the story of Coach Paul 'Bear' Bryant, a highly successful and respected US college football coach in his book, *The Millionaire Mind*. At a seminar for senior executives, Stanley asked one of Coach Bryant's former players to share the first thing Coach Bryant said when he arrived on campus.

The player said that Coach Bryant's first words had taken everyone by surprise: 'Have you called your folks yet to thank them?' Then he followed this up with this: 'No one ever got to this level without the help of others. Call your folks. Thank them.'

Your associations build you. Your associations make you. As the great US athletics star Wilma Rudolph once said, 'No matter what great things you accomplish, somebody helps you.' No matter how successful we become, we will always need other people to help us continue to progress. Even Tiger Woods spends time with a coach every day.

Every level of success will bring you into higher associations. So don't ever think that you have 'made it,' and that you no longer need support or help from those around you. No matter what you have achieved or how successful you are, there will be others out there who have something to offer you. Find these people and continue to learn and grow.

Stretch your comfort zone

To get to a higher level of association, you sometimes have to stretch your comfort zone. Sometimes we can be afraid of going to another level because it might mean losing current associations and friends. The fact is, every new level of success will always bring us into a new level of relationships and associations.

Your associations build you. Your associations make you.

Some time ago, I had the privilege of meeting the prime minister of Australia. I was attending a function with a whole lot of other people, including a number of my own friends and acquaintances. When I arrived, I found that I had been seated at a table with the Prime Minister and some special guests. My friends were all seated at another table in another room.

I have to admit that I felt uncomfortable meeting the prime minister. I was more comfortable being with people I knew, but I had to understand that to meet the prime minister — someone who operates at a higher level of leadership, influence and power — was an opportunity to be grasped. I knew I had to stretch myself to go outside my comfort zone. Once I decided to flow with the opportunity, it turned out to be a most enjoyable experience.

Add value to others

One of the greatest keys to prosperity is to add value to people. In your relationships, be the one who brings things to the relationship. Bring wisdom, bring insight, bring your time, bring your commitment...because if you do, your life will prosper. As my great friend Dr Robb Thompson once said, 'The prophecy of your future lies in the relationships of today.'

Challenge:
Build connections to people who believe in you

Think about the people in your world and identify who is important to you. Who are your mentors and role models? Who are your most important peers—the people you can share your life with and who will support, encourage and believe in you?

If you find that you are lacking meaningful associations, start identifying some people who you think you need to get closer to and take whatever steps are necessary to build your connections with them today.

Chapter 15

Aim for the stars

Dreams are a catalyst for releasing extraordinary achievements and prosperity. In 1982, at the official opening of the newly completed Epcot Center at Disney World in Florida, one of the Disney executives turned to Walt Disney's widow, Lillian, and said, 'If only Walt could have seen this!'

'He did,' she replied, 'That's why it's here.' Before anything significant manifests itself, it always starts as a dream.

A dream is an intangible picture from which you create a tangible future. The extent of your prosperity will be constrained by the size of your dream. To develop a millionaire mindset, you need to become a big dreamer, a big thinker. Georgia State University professor David Schwartz said, 'Where success is concerned, people are not measured in inches or pounds or college degrees or family backgrounds; they are measured by the size of their thinking.' Or, as Donald Trump put it, 'You have to think anyway, so why not think big?'

When someone like Jack Welch, the once great leader of General Electric, said that an ongoing relationship with a customer is more important than the sale of an individual product, he was focusing on the big picture. What is the big picture in your area of work or business? Is it product, profitability or people? It may be none or all of those three. Understand what the big picture is, because it's the big picture that will create wealth and motivation.

> If you live with a small view of things, you are putting a lid on your progress and your prosperity.

Playwright Victor Hugo observed, 'A small man is made up of small thoughts.' To develop a millionaire mindset you have got to learn to think big—to have a big view of the world, a big view of life, a big view of yourself and a big view of others. If you live with a small view of things, you are putting a lid on your progress and your prosperity.

What's your dream?

One day a friend of mine was driving to the golf course with his 12-year-old son. In the car with them that day was my friend's father, the boy's grandfather. Two different mindsets were on display in that car. The grandfather was a man who was not given to a positive or prosperous mindset. He was, as they say, from the old school. In contrast, my friend and his son had fed their minds on a steady diet of personal development. As a result, my friend's son was such a positive young man that he was regularly winning golf tournaments alongside others who were two to three years older than he was. He won his first prestigious golf tournament at the age of 12 in a field of 15-year-olds.

While driving in the car, my friend said to his son, 'Tell Grandpa what you want to be one day.'

'Grandpa,' said the boy, 'I want to win the US Open one day.'

In shock and horror, the grandfather said to his son, 'How can you let him think that? You know he's never going to win the US Open! Why would you give this kid false hope?'

My friend turned to his father and said, 'Dad, if he shoots for the stars, he may just hit the moon, but at least he will have left the Earth!'

How easy it is to find those people who will sap you of your dreams, sap you of your goals, and your hope. They surround us in a circle of pessimism and cynicism. Sure, you may never become a multimillionaire, but you may just become a millionaire! You may not win the US Open, but you may win 10 other international tournaments, travel to the world's best golf courses and befriend some of the most successful golfers in your time. Aim high, because then you're bound to hit something. Likewise, if you aim low, you're bound to hit something, but it won't be a happy sight! Only one of those two aims will give you a greater sense of fulfillment and purpose. Only one of those two aims is a great motivator.

If you are committed to a millionaire mindset and to a philosophy of abundance, then you've got to create a big mentality. Most people want a $100 000 income with a $5 mentality and that will never happen. Even if it does, with a small, poverty mindset your income will soon shrink back to the level of your mindset.

I once asked a woman in a mentoring program I was running, 'Deborah, what's your dream?'

'I don't know,' she said. 'Can you tell me?'

I had to laugh. So many people have no clarity of vision; no clear purpose. As I have said before, if there's a mist in your head, then there's a fog over your life. You've got to have a dream — a dream can only come true for you if you have one!

Once during an interview Paul McCartney was asked how he came to write his famous song *Yesterday*. 'I dreamed it,' he said. He actually woke up one morning with the tune in his head. As he ate breakfast that morning he put the following words to the tune: 'Scrambled egg. How I love to eat a scrambled egg.' Later he put a little more thought into the lyrics and the rest, as they say, is history.

I recently watched the great Australian champion fighter Kostya Tszyu lose a fight to UK boxer Ricky Hatton. I later learned that this defeat had started a long time before the fight, after Tszyu had won a world title fight.

A young Hatton — who had only fought a few professional fights at the time — jumped into the ring and said to Tszyu, 'I have a dream that one day I'm going to fight you for the world title.' That was his dream, which has now been fulfilled.

Nothing of consequence ever happens without a dream. People who do not have a dream about their future do not know where they are heading. But dreamers know where they are heading; they know where their future lies. They aim strategically and, like an arrow hitting its target, they will hit their desired goal.

Every great achievement begins with a dream. Henry Ford dreamt that lots of people would one day drive an affordable car. Martin Luther King Jr changed an entire nation and inspired generations around the world with the words, 'I have a dream.'

A millionaire mind dreams big

How big can you dream? What limitations are you putting on yourself, your prosperity and your wealth? A millionaire mind is a mind that dreams big. If the dream is big enough, the facts don't matter. The key to your prosperity lies in the seed of your dream. James Allen, author of *As a Man Thinketh*, said, 'Dreams are the seedlings of reality.' There is nothing more powerful than a dream. Best-selling author Tom Clancy once said, 'Nothing is as real as a dream. The world will change around you, but your dream will not.' No matter what happens, nobody can take your dream away from you as long as you are determined to hold onto it.

> What limitations are you putting on yourself, your prosperity and your wealth?

They had a dream

A study conducted by Harvard physiologist David McClelland discovered that high achievers and successful people have one important characteristic in common: they fantasise and dream incessantly about how to achieve their goals. Here are some examples:

- After his older brother was shot down and killed in World War II, Dick Clark would listen to the radio for hours to ease his painful loneliness. He began dreaming of someday becoming an announcer with his own radio show. The result of Clark's dream was the hugely successful show *American Bandstand*.

- Two brothers-in-law started their own business and advertised a single product served 31 different ways. Their dream was to make $75 a week. Today, Baskin-Robbins is a dream come true, not only for its founders, but also for ice-cream lovers everywhere!

- The Bank of America exists today because AP Giannini, a high school dropout, dreamed of starting a financial institution that served the little guy. By making previously unheard-of automobile and appliance loans, his dream had become a reality by the time of his death in 1949.

- American cyclist Lance Armstrong dreamed that one day he would win the Tour de France. He has won that famous event seven times — and will try for an eighth time in 2009!

- Walt Disney had a dream to build a theme park. What started as a scribbly little mouse went on to become one of the biggest and most successful entertainment empires in the world today.

It costs nothing to dream

It costs nothing to dream, but it will cost you not to have one. As Dr Robert Schuller said, 'Since it doesn't cost a dime to dream, you should never short-change yourself when you stretch your imagination.'

Woodrow Wilson said:

> *All big men are dreamers. They see things in the soft haze of a spring day or in the red fire of a long winter's evening. Some of us let these great dreams die, but others nourish and protect them; nurse them through bad days till they bring them to the sunshine and light, which comes always to those who sincerely hope that their dreams will come true.*

Between yesterday's dream and tomorrow's regret is today's opportunity. You need to capitalise on today's opportunities. Make the most of every opportunity that comes your way. See opportunities as the path to the fulfillment of your dream. A dream must generate action; otherwise it will never become a reality. What actions can you take right now to cause your dreams to become reality?

Your dream determines your behaviour

You must believe the dream. To grow into reality, an extraordinary dream must be fed. Your dream should determine your conduct and behaviour. Your dream should lead you to make appointments that will foster its fulfillment. Your dream will give birth to changes in your relationships and create brand new habits for success and wealth. Dreams are generally birthed by a deep desire for change, for something to be better than it is. Your dream will give birth to extraordinary passion that dominates your consciousness and thoughts.

A dream must generate action; otherwise it will never become a reality.

Although dreams are free, the fulfillment of a dream will require sacrifice. Look at anyone who has seen their dream fulfilled and you'll see that it has always cost them something — Martin Luther King Jr had a dream, but it cost him his life. It may cost you friendship, it may cost you a change of thinking — it may cost you a whole lot of things, but any dream worth pursuing is worth its price.

It's amazing how many people allow their dreams to be shattered just because they face a few challenges or obstacles. We all have challenges. We all have issues. I know I do! Here's a fact of life: Right now, you are either leaving a crisis or are about to enter one. The fulfillment of dreams involves heartaches, struggles and challenges. That's what makes it so worthwhile when your dream is achieved.

Money follows vision

I remember how at the age of 17 I had a vision of my life. I didn't even fully understand it at the time. All I could see was a sea of faces of young people and I knew I would one day be speaking into their lives. I heard a little voice inside me say, 'You can build this!' I remember going to a youth convention that was so boring that even boring people called it boring! I looked at that youth convention and thought, *I could take this over one day and make it better!*

What would happen if even 20 per cent of your dream came to pass?

Some time later, I started my first event with a crowd of 350 young people and no budget.

I have found in life that lack of money is never really the problem—*lack of vision* is the issue. I've never had enough money to do the things I wanted. But I've found that money follows vision. If you do have the money, it simply means the vision isn't big enough.

After my first event, I lost about 180 people because they didn't agree with what I was doing. But I had a vision. I knew what I wanted to do. At my next event I had 300 people, then 500, then 800, then 1000, then 1200... Soon I was packing the Sydney Town Hall. Then we packed out Sydney's 5000-seat Hordern Pavilion, then the State Sports Centre, which holds 7000. Next, I set my sights on the 12 000-seat Sydney Entertainment Centre.

I remember walking into the empty Sydney Entertainment Centre one day and saying to myself, 'I'm going to fill this building!' I went on to fill it seven times.

I had more young people turning up to my events than most rock concerts. After that, I went to the Parramatta Football Stadium, a large outdoor sports arena in the heart of Sydney. People were still asking me, 'Where will you get the money? How will you do it?' To be honest, I didn't have a clue. We can be too dependent on clues. Sometimes our problem is that we think we need to know exactly how it is going to be done instead of believing in our dream and in ourselves. Sometimes you just have to have a go. You just have to go out and do it.

Don't just dream it — do it!

Of course, the whole point of having a dream is to see that dream fulfilled. Hyatt Resorts once had a slogan that said, *Having your dreams fulfilled can be more therapeutic than having them analysed.* Don't spend your whole life analysing your dream — fulfill it! Don't let anyone else analyse your dream and tear it to bits. Don't expect anyone else to understand your dream — it is *your* dream, not theirs. Your dream is about your future, not your present. Don't allow so-called 'experts' to rob you of your dream.

Follow the dream. Follow your heart and your vision. As much as we need to have a plan, we can spend too much time sitting around analysing and over-planning. What is ultimately important is the dream and the vision. So when the plan fails or things don't go according to plan, the vision is still alive. It's the vision, not the plan, that keeps us going. I love that old Elvis song where he follows that dream. You may ask, 'What happens if it doesn't work?' But what if it does? What would happen if even 20 per cent of your dream came to pass?

Without a dream or a vision you will get to the end of your life and wonder what could have been. Everybody ends up somewhere in life. You can either end up somewhere on purpose or just end up wherever you allow life to take you. If you don't have a vision for your life, then you will have no control over your destination.

How do you want to be remembered? You don't want written on your gravestone, 'She kept a clean house.' What do you want on your gravestone? 'Here lies a coulda, shoulda, woulda…' What do you want said about *you*? One day, these words could describe your legacy: 'Here lies a dreamer. He dared to dream!

'Impossible' is an opinion.

In 1866, Alfred Nobel invented dynamite as a result of trying to make nitro-glycerine safer to handle. Although he hadn't invented dynamite with a view to it being used in warfare, this soon became the case. Nobel later became involved in the development of weaponry, but he also maintained an ideological commitment to peace. It has been said that the reason he instituted the Nobel Peace Prize was that he wanted his primary legacy to the world to be the promotion of peace, not war.

'Impossible' is an opinion

Many people will say to you, 'It can't be done!' or 'You don't have what it takes!' Plenty of people will find reasons to dismiss your dream. The millionaire mindset is not shaken by the negative opinions of critics. For every major achievement in history, there would have been someone somewhere saying it couldn't be done—that it was impossible.

Let me say a few things about the word *impossible*. It is a word that reflects a small mindset. To the millionaire mindset, this word is not a declaration—it's a dare. *'Impossible' is an opinion*. It does not have to be a fact. At the time John F Kennedy announced that man would one day walk on the moon, it was technologically impossible to achieve. But even though JFK never lived to see the fulfillment of his vision, that day he created a big picture in the mindsets of the American people and the impossible became possible.

At one stage they said it was impossible to run a mile in under four minutes. Now, you could not even qualify for the Olympic Games if you can't run a mile under four minutes. By declaring something *impossible*, somebody with a small mindset dares someone else to live in the big picture.

No vision means no progress

When people have no vision for the future, they tend to do three things:

- They revert to their past.

- They spend all their time making excuses to explain why their lives are going nowhere.

- They stop living and settle for merely existing.

When I was running my drug rehabilitation program, many of the boys in our program had no real vision for their lives beyond getting out of the program. All they wanted to do was to get clean and quit drugs. Human nature is such that unless a person has a clear picture of their future, they will always return to their past. While these boys had no vision for their futures, I could pretty much guarantee that even if they left our program clean, it would only be a matter of time before they reverted back into their old habits.

If you don't have a dream for your life, someone else will have one for you. When I was a kid, my father used to say to me, 'Son, when you get bigger, you're going to be a doctor.' So I never got bigger! And anyway, that wasn't my dream, it was my father's.

Some of us can easily be carried along by other people's dreams — including our partner's dreams for us — but it's your dream, not theirs, that is important. Nobody should rob you of your dream, especially if they love you. If someone really loves you, then they'll love everything about you, including your dreams, which they may not really understand or agree with. If they truly love you, they should say, 'Well, if that makes you happy, if that's what you want to do, I'll support you, I'll help you make it happen.'

How will your dream come true?

To escape the past, you need to create your future today... and it starts with a dream. Stephen Covey once stated, 'Begin with the end in mind.' Without a vision for your future, you'll reach the end of your life and look back and wonder what could have been if things had been different. You will find yourself always talking about the 'good old days' and regretting what you might have become. There is nothing more tragic than hearing someone in their latter years utter the words, 'If only...' And there is nothing more inspiring than seeing a person near the end of their life able to look back and declare, 'I did it! I finished the race. I achieved what I set out to do.'

What will you be saying at the end of your life? What is your vision for the next year, two years, five years and 10 years? Your future has to start as a picture in your head today. What's your vision? How will your dream come true?

Challenge:
See past your today to your tomorrow

What's your dream?
What do you see in your future? Don't
focus on where you are right now. You need to
see beyond what is now to what could be and what
should be. All of us should have a vision for our wealth,
for our health, for our families, for the people we can
influence, and for our businesses or careers. What is in
your heart of hearts? What is the thing that you long
to do in your wildest dreams? How big is it? How
big can you make this thing called your 'life'?

Chapter 16

Fuel your dream with passion

In chapter 14, we looked at establishing your dream and your vision. There is no such thing as a vision void of emotion. Even the most routine activities feel good when they are undertaken in order to fulfill your dream that is fuelled by passion. Life is so much more rewarding if you have passion. I'm passionate and emotional about everything—I'd cry at the opening of a shopping centre!

You've got to be passionate in your pursuit of prosperity for it to be successful. Without passion, you will never possess what you pursue. Pursuit and passion go hand in hand. The proof of your desire to prosper is in your passionate pursuit.

I am involved in many Third World programs. My wife and I help to feed and educate children in some of the most desolate areas of the world. I've observed that the childrens' discontent with their current status pushes them to excel in the midst of the poverty that surrounds them. It is amazing and inspiring to see that many of them see themselves as prosperous in their own culture. They don't wear gold watches. They don't drive expensive cars. They don't even own television sets. But what they do have is an abundant prosperity mentality. They place a high value on what they already have and on what is given to them. They keep their clothes and their homes very clean, they value a gift when it is given to them. And they have a driving, contagious passion to move out of poverty into prosperity.

What are you passionate about?

During a meeting in South Africa some years ago, I heard the brilliant author and speaker Robert Kiyosaki define passion as *the tension that exists between something you love and something you hate*. I'm passionate about seeing people become wealthy. I love seeing people become prosperous and succeeding in life.

Equally, I hate seeing people broke and imprisoned by poverty. My passion exists in the tension I feel between the things I love and the things I hate. I am passionate about shifting people's mindsets away from poverty to prosperity. I find myself thinking, *If you could just see what I see!*

I remember a time when I had to confront a senior political figure in my home state about the issue of drug addiction. I was spitting mad and he could see it in my eyes. I get emotional about peoples' addictions to drugs and the strategies governments employ to deal with the problem. I passionately do not believe in harm minimisation — it doesn't work. I was running a drug rehabilitation program with an 86 per cent success rate and the state government was opening shooting galleries for drug addicts.

I was so mad, but I directed my anger towards a positive and productive end: I decided to prove them wrong.

I'm also passionate about young kids being dealt antidepressants at six and seven years of age. As far as I'm concerned, that's wrong. Maybe they just need a friend and a mentor.

What are you passionate about? What motivates you? What really fires you up? How can this help you pursue your dream? You have to get emotional about your dream, to feel something about it. There will be obstacles along the way and you will need this passion to overcome them.

> You have to get emotional about your dream, to feel something about it.

Do you get emotional about what you believe in? Do you get emotional about your wealth? Do you get emotional about your business? Are you emotionally attached to what you do? You see, you cannot be emotionally detached from what you do and expect to be successful. Your soul is the seat of your emotions. Remember Aristotle's dictum: the soul can't think without a picture. The picture of your dream in your soul should stir you emotionally; if there's no emotion attached to your dream, it remains lifeless.

When someone is passionate about what they do, their passion rubs off on the people around them. The difference between being bored and excited by something someone is telling you has less to do with your interest in the subject than the level of passion with which the information is related.

I'll say it again: dreams and vision have to involve emotion; the clearer your vision, the stronger your emotions will be.

Do what you love and love what you do

You've got to do what you love and love what you do. If you will learn that simple key, your life will prosper. Why?

Because you will never prosper in something you don't love. If a husband and wife don't love each other, how can that relationship prosper? If you don't love creating wealth and abundance, how can you prosper? An emotion such as love is a powerful motivating factor for every human being on this planet. When you love what you do, it's no longer a job — it's a love, a passion and a pursuit, and success will follow that passionate pursuit.

...your prosperity is more than likely going to flow out of your strengths and gifts.

When it comes to developing a millionaire mindset, you have to love your dream and love what you are doing to make your dream a reality. If you don't love what you are doing, then do something else! Vision is always emotional. Everyone has a different vision because everyone gets excited by different things. I have friends who have a great vision for their computer business. I have no vision for computers — I don't even like the things! But when my friends speak about what they can do with computers and technology, it is almost as though they are speaking about the person that they want to spend the rest of their life with. They are passionate about their vision; they are enthused and it motivates them.

There is usually a strong correlation between what you are passionate about and what you are good at doing. That means your prosperity is more than likely going to flow out of your strengths and gifts. You'll never create wealth from projects you're not good at or projects you don't enjoy. I'm yet to meet a person who became wealthy doing something they don't enjoy. If you don't enjoy what you're doing in your business or your work right now, you probably won't become prosperous doing that. You can't have two diametrically opposed thoughts about the same thing and expect to be successful.

In his book *Cure for the Common Life*, best-selling author Max Lucado claims most people are sick of the way they live their lives. He says that one-third of Americans say, 'I hate my job.' He also reveals that 70 per cent of Americans publicly admit no enthusiasm or passion for their work. A similar percentage of people are in the wrong career because it doesn't match their abilities and preferences. If you don't enjoy the job you're in right now, it's highly unlikely that you'll ever become wealthy from it. My advice to you is to do something else. As the saying goes, 'Find a job you love and you'll never work another day in your life.'

I know I will never get wealthy doing administrative work or developing computer programs. I don't know a thing about them and I have no passion for them. Singing is not my gift either. I was in the car with my wife one day when Michael Bolton came on the radio singing *How Am I Supposed to Live Without You?* I started singing along with Michael, directing the words of the song at my wife, but quickly stopped when she said, 'Shut up, or you'll find out!'

My gift is definitely not singing. My gift is speaking, teaching, inspiring and motivating people. There are days when I get tired of doing what I do, but I still love it. I love speaking. (Whether people love listening to me is another matter!) I love producing books and CDs and putting them into people's hands and saying, 'Okay, go get rich!'

Create wealth from your position of strength

What is your gift? You will create prosperity out of your gift. You will always create wealth from your position of strength. How many times have you heard someone tell you that you need to figure out your gift and work on your weaknesses? What a load of nonsense!

Michael Jordan was a great basketball player who retired from basketball to try his hand at baseball. But no matter how much he focused on it, he was never going to be great. On the basketball court, though, he was a superhero. If the Bulls were down by two points with five seconds to go, the coach would call time-out and no matter what instructions he might have been giving the team, everybody knew that there was one guy who was going to get the ball: Michael Jordan. Focus on your gift; work on your strengths.

Vision has to involve passion and motiv-ation. You can always identify motivated people because they are passionate. The *Collins Dictionary* defines passion as 'eagerness, excitement, fervour, fire, heat, intensity, rapture, joy, spirit, zest and zeal'. Does that describe how you feel about creating prosperity in your life? Does that describe how you feel about the vision you have for your life?

Passion is not nebulous; it is always directed at something. It is generally directed at a vision of how things can and should be. Vision is born out of concern. What stirs you up? What moves you? What drives you to action? For many years I have been passionate about helping people become self-managed and self-motivated. I am passionate about helping people discover and release their capacity to create wealth. Why? Because I believe in the power of free enterprise. I am passionate about being a compassionate capitalist! In other words, I have prosperity for a purpose. My money, your money, our money can accomplish great things. With money, we can make the world a better place.

Passion is born out of concern

All my passion is born out of a concern for something. I am even passionate about food — especially Italian food! I become greatly disturbed and concerned when people don't cook Italian food the way it ought to be cooked!

Some time ago I was dining at one of my favourite Italian restaurants in Sydney. The owner, who recently celebrated his 50th year in business, told me how he had recently been to another Italian restaurant.

His words were, 'How could they cook food like that?' He was disgusted at how some Italian restaurants produce the great dishes that come from Italy. He was passionate because he was concerned; passion and concern are two sides of the same coin.

When your dream is infused with passion, even the most mundane aspects of fulfilling your dream become meaningful. Everybody has to do mundane things on a day-to-day basis. No dream becomes a reality without a considerable amount of routine, menial work. A dream can transform even the most tedious task into a goal-directed activity.

Imagine that you work in a factory that produces sandbags. Imagine if all you had to do all day, every day, was fill bags with sand. How boring would that be?

Now imagine that your home and everything you own is under threat from rising flood waters and the only way you can save your home is by building walls around your home with bags of sand. Under those circumstances, filling sandbags would become your obsession. You'd throw everything you had into it! The difference is that now your emotions are engaged and you have a vision — to see your home survive the flood. Vision gives significance to the mundane. You do whatever you have to do to get you to where you want to go. You do it with enthusiasm because it is all about fulfilling your personal dream.

One of the things I find mundane is flying. I really hate flying, whatever class of ticket I might have. But when I get to my destination, it's a different story. I'm thinking about who might be in the meeting. It could be the next Bill Gates. There could be someone there who is going to change the world. I remember one day a man invited me to come and speak at an event he had organised with about 7000 people attending. When I got to the event, I was impressed.

'Who inspired you to do this?' I asked him.

'I was at a youth camp years ago and you were the speaker. I came up to you during the camp and asked you how I could build a big organisation like yours. You looked at me and said, "Son, get a dream and work your butt off." And that's what I did. So that's why I wanted you to be the speaker at my first big event.'

Mundane tasks are mandatory to your success

Recently I was working with a group of real estate professionals and I asked them to identify one of the most mundane activities that they had to do in the course of their jobs. Someone replied, 'Answering the phone.'

I would have thought that answering the phone is quite important in real estate — as in any business. I pointed out that one of the great lessons in sales success is that if you don't ring, your phone doesn't ring. Another basic axiom of business is this: when the phone rings, answer it. It may seem a mundane task, but it is mandatory to your success and the profitability of your organisation, which makes it meaningful.

Don't let disappointment stop you

Of course, the potential downside of being passionate is that it leaves you open to disappointment when things don't go according to plan. If there's no passion, you rarely get disappointed because you don't really care.

But when you care, you can experience the downside of passion. All of us have disappointments in our lives. The answer is to ensure that your vision always exceeds your disappointment quota. If it's the other way around, then your disappointments will overtake your vision.

How do you ensure your vision quota always stays above your disappointment quota? It's largely a matter of managing expectations. Disappointment comes from unmet expectations. Don't get disappointed with yourself by putting unreasonable expectations on yourself. I expect a high standard of myself in a lot of areas, but I also know there are some things I'm not good at, so I don't put unrealistic expectations on myself in those areas. I don't allow myself to be disappointed about certain things. Above all, you have to keep believing — no matter what. You have to believe that dreams come true.

Challenge:
Develop a passion for prosperity

What are you concerned about? What flicks your switch? What makes you angry? What makes you exuberant? What drives you? What makes you burn with fervour? This is not about feelings—this is a disposition you need to have to increase your prosperity. You need to develop a passionate disposition about creating wealth for yourself and for others.

Chapter 17

Fuel your passion with a reason

Why do you want to prosper? What's your ultimate motivation? My firm belief is that your ultimate purpose needs to be bigger than yourself. Your passion needs to be directed outward towards other people. If the only thing we are passionate about is ourselves, then our desire for prosperity is nothing more than an expression of narcissism. Ultimately, your pursuit of wealth needs to be altruistically motivated. Your over-arching attitude should not be 'What's in it for me?', but rather, 'What's in it for them?' You need to ask yourself, 'What value am I to others?' Go for a win-win every time—if they win, you win!

My own passion—my *why*—is born out of a general concern for humanity and, specifically, a concern for broken people. I am passionate about helping those who have no voice to discover a voice for themselves. I am passionately opposed to drug abuse. I am passionate about my friends' success. I am concerned that people should not have to rely on handouts to survive in the future. We must have a vision to create our own wealth.

We need to understand that our success is linked to the success of the people around us. Nobody ever becomes a millionaire by themselves. If I can make life better for other people, it will make my life better. And if I can help the people around me become successful, then their success becomes my success. In a very real way, my income is the direct result of how many people I help. If the number one motivation in your life is to accept responsibility for adding value to the lives of other people, then everything else will fall into place.

> In a very real way, my income is the direct result of how many people I help.

When the late actor Paul Newman and his friend AE Hotchner started their famous 'Paul Newman's Own' brand of salad dressing in 1980, they made a commitment to donate all the profits after tax to charity. The company donated over $1 million in its first year of operation. To date they have donated more than $200 million to a range of charities and aid organisations. They knew what their *why* was.

Learn to give

A true millionaire mindset is always focused on the 'why' of success, which often revolves around the needs of other people. A few years ago, I was helping out a youth program in Eastern Europe. One night I was out buying some dinner for some of the kids and I saw one young man take his burger, cut it in half, wrap one half in his serviette and put it in his pocket. I said to him, 'Hey, buddy! You don't have to hang on to that. We can buy some more burgers later.'

He replied that it wasn't for him, it was for his sister, who hadn't eaten in days. Despite his own hunger, his first impulse was to share. His sister didn't know he had a burger, so she would have been none the wiser if he'd eaten the whole thing, but he put his sister's need before his own. That's a millionaire mindset.

You have probably heard the saying, 'Give and it shall be given to you.' Most of us would rightly agree that giving is a virtuous act. The prosperous person is a giver, but the prosperous person also knows how to receive. We need to become transmitters of wealth; a transmitter receives input and then sends it out again. In the same way, we need to be able to receive before we can give. The poor can't help the poor because they are poor. It is a prosperous person, a person of abundance, a flourishing person who can be a transmitter of wealth. To become this kind of person, you've got to first learn to be a receiver.

First learn to receive

Once you decide to be a receiver, you will attract what you are willing to receive. Some people constantly attract trouble because they are willing to receive it. In all my years of working in drug rehabilitation and with young people, I have only once been offered drugs — and that was when I was on holiday! I choose not to receive that environment around me, therefore, I don't attract it. Trouble can be everywhere around me, but I choose not to receive it. What are you choosing to receive?

What are you allowing into your life that you don't want? Some people receive negativity and gossip because they choose to receive these things. I choose not to.

You need to develop your capacity to receive the things you want to receive into your life. When you receive compliments, do you put on false humility or do you receive it with thanks? When you receive money, do you feel like you need to apologise for it or feel bad about it?

If you do, then you are putting a lid on your prosperity. These responses reflect a sense of unworthiness. When you receive wealth, you need to be comfortable with it — embrace it, acknowledge it and enjoy it.

To be a bigger receiver, you need a bigger capacity.

How much you can receive is limited by how 'big' you are. A jar can contain only so much. A house can only contain so much. But a warehouse can contain so much more. To be a bigger receiver, you need a bigger capacity. The artist James Baillie said, 'To grow and know what one is growing towards — that is the source of all strength and confidence in life.' To grow and know that I am growing towards being a receiver with a capacity for prosperity brings a strength and dignity to my life that I could never have with a limited mindset.

People who believe in themselves, no matter who they are, stand on a higher level and have a greater capacity than a people who are unsure of who they are and what they believe in. To be a receiver means you will stand out. To be prosperous means you will live at a higher level. The great Presbyterian minister William JH Boetcker said this:

> It has always been a crime to be above the crowd. That's the real reason why some in public life are maligned, attacked and slandered, for they are beyond the reach of those who realise in their own heart that the greatness of others shows their own smallness and their own inferiority.

Successful people care about the needs of others

A worthwhile vision will always show care and concern for people. Any great visionary is a person who cares about other people and their needs. In the USA, there's a department store called Nordstrom. A friend of mine took me there one day. He said, 'Pat, you need to come and experience Nordstrom. Talk about customer service — you won't believe it! I'm going to take this pair of shoes back.'

I said, 'You're kidding! But you're wearing them!'

He said, 'That's right. And I'm taking them back. They'll give me another pair of shoes, no questions asked.'

We walked into the store and approached the sales desk. My friend explained that the shoes were not fitting well and that he wanted to exchange them for a new pair. (The shoes were worth about $400.)

The sales assistant's immediate reply was, 'Yes, sir. No problem at all.' He then looked up my friend's customer details — including his shoe size — and asked if he would like another pair of black shoes. My friend decided he would prefer a brown pair, so the assistant went back to the storeroom and came out with a new pair of brown shoes. My friend tried them on and was happy.

> How much you can receive is limited by how 'big' you are.

The assistant thanked him for his custom. 'Always a pleasure to serve you, Mr Smith,' he said.

As we left the store, I said to my friend, 'Do you always bring your old shoes back here and get a new pair?'

'No,' he replied. 'I just wanted to show you what a great store this is. I buy all my clothes at Nordstrom because their policy is that the customer always comes first — and they mean it.'

One day, a 'bag lady' — unwashed, smelly and shabbily dressed — walked into a Nordstrom store and went straight to a department that sold expensive dresses. She walked up to a sales assistant and said, 'I want to buy a dress. Not just any dress — I want a nice one. I'm going to a party and I want a nice dress to wear. I have money, you know.'

The sales assistant politely replied, 'No problem, ma'am. What size are you?'

'I don't know,' the woman replied.

So the assistant took her to a fitting area and measured her up and then began bringing her dresses worth $500, $800 and $1500 for her to try on. Eventually she picked one she liked and the sales assistant asked, 'Would you like some shoes to go with that?'

'Yes,' the woman replied. 'I do need shoes. And not just some cheap shoes — I'm going to a party and I want to look nice. I have money, you know.'

So the assistant helped her out of her boots and came back with several pairs of expensive shoes. The assistant fitted her and helped her select a pair. The assistant then went on to help her select some nice jewellery to go with her outfit. Then she said, 'Why don't we do something with your hair as well?'

The woman's hair was unwashed and matted. So the assistant took her to the hairdressing department and they washed her hair, cut it and put it up in a bun. When they were finished, the assistant showed the woman a mirror and said, 'There, don't you look lovely?'

The woman looked at herself and replied, 'Take it all off. I don't like it.'

So they took everything off. She left without buying a thing. But before she left the store, the assistant gave her a card and said, 'Thank you for visiting us here at Nordstrom today. It was a pleasure serving you. This is my name and my number. If you ever have any needs that I can help with, please feel free to call me at any time.'

A few weeks later, an article appeared in a major US newspaper entitled 'My experience at Nordstrom'. The bag lady had been an undercover reporter who had gone to the store to test whether their commitment to customer service lived up to the promise. That sales assistant became very popular on the speaking circuit. She became quite wealthy as a result of the way she had performed that day.

When you treat people well, it unlocks the potential for wealth. People bring you money. But your vision must have the wellbeing of other people at its core.

Don't let your prosperity be hindered by other people's small-mindedness

Never let your prosperity be hindered by other people's inferiority and small mindedness. Never let other people hinder your capacity to receive. Your capacity to receive will always show up the smallness and limitations of others. As Ralph Waldo Emerson said, 'To be great is to be misunderstood.' If you desire prosperity and an increase in prosperity, you will be misunderstood. People who are going nowhere, doing nothing and achieving little are left alone, but once you choose to flourish, abound, increase and prosper, you face attack from all directions — from friends, colleagues and especially those who have no capacity to receive.

When you treat people well, it unlocks the potential for wealth.

The Greyhound bus company's motto used to be: 'When dealing in basic human need you will always be needed.' If you want to be wealthy, you should focus your vision on dealing in basic human need. When our purpose is to meet needs, we are living for something beyond ourselves. How are you meeting needs in the lives of others? What are you doing to help other people belong, to be financially secure and to have a sense of achievement? If you can deal in these three basic human needs, if your vision is to help people belong and be accepted, be financially secure and find a sense of achievement, then you are on your way to developing a millionaire mindset.

If you are meeting human needs, then all you have to do is help people to see that you are meeting their need. The reason people are prepared to pay me to do what I do is because I am meeting a need in them. If I wasn't meeting some need, then no matter how clever or articulate I might be, nobody would want to hear from me.

Challenge:
Develop purpose and prosperity will follow

So, why do you want to prosper? What ultimately motivates you? What is your purpose for success? You need to have an ultimate purpose bigger than yourself. If you don't have a purpose, go and search for one. Without a purpose, your passion will wane.

Here's my challenge to you: whatever you want, give it away—it will come back to you. If you want love, give love. If you want happiness, give happiness. If you want money, give it away. Money is like a seed. There's a law in life called the law of seed time and harvest. It's a universal law that has always been around and always will. According to this law, if you sow something of value, it will grow and return to you in increased measure. Focus on others, and others will focus on you.

Conclusion

I started this book by saying that I'm on a mission to help make people rich. I want to help make you rich, but first you've got to adopt a millionaire mindset. There is a reason why the rich get richer and the poor get poorer. Generally it has to do with mindsets. Some scientists once created a scenario in which all the wealth of the world was distributed equally amongst everybody. In other words, in this scenario you and I would have received a share of Bill Gates's money! The conclusion they came to was that every time they performed this scenario, the wealth would always return to the original owners. Why? The rich have a mindset that the poor don't have.

One of the early pioneers of Christianity, the apostle Paul, once wrote, 'Do not conform any longer to the pattern of this world, but be transformed by the renewing of your mind.' That's essentially what this book is all about. Do not allow yourself to go through life simply conforming to the patterns of thinking and living that are dictated to you by the world. You could easily blame your upbringing, your education, negative social norms or statements that may have been said about you for your situation. How should you respond to these issues? *Transform your life by the renewal of your mind.*

In the 1979 film *Being There*, the late Peter Sellers played the main character: a gardener named Chance who had lived his entire life in an old mansion in the middle of Washington, DC. Chance had never been outside the owner's property, spending every day tending the small walled garden attached to the house. Apart from limited contact with a housekeeper who came to the house each day to cook and clean, his only knowledge of the outside world was based on what he had seen on television, which he watched almost continually.

When the owner of the mansion died, for the first time in his life Chance had to leave the only home he had ever known and venture out into the outside world. The rest of the film is about how Chance survived in this big new world, interpreting and responding to every situation in which he found himself by relating it to what he had seen on television or to his knowledge of gardening.

The final line of the film is, 'Life is a state of mind.' While that sentiment might be a little too existentialist for me, it is certainly true to say that the path of your life will be determined to a large extent by the state of your mind. Remember, if there's a mist in your mind, there will be a fog surrounding your world.

So, as you begin today to change your mindset, the mist in your mind will begin to clear. And as the mist clears, the fog surrounding your world will lift ever so gently. As that happens, you'll find yourself beginning to see further than you've ever seen before. New horizons of opportunity and possibility will appear before you. Paths of prosperity that once eluded you now stretch out before you. Rivers of riches now flow within your reach. Gardens of greatness are now at your fingertips. With the dawn of each new day, you'll awake to the realisation that your dreams are achievable.

The difference between yesterday and tomorrow is simply that you have decided to apply a millionaire mindset. And that will make *all* the difference!

Reference #

Your FREE special gifts from Pat Mesiti

As a special reward for finishing this book, I would like to take you to the next level.

Claim these two very special offers by emailing **events@mesiti.com** with your name, address and phone number.

Special Offer No.1
Receive **TWO FREE TICKETS** to our **3 Day Wealth Creation Live Events** Valued at $997
Take your business, your relationships and yourself to a whole new level!

Special Offer No.2
You've read the book and now you want to transform your car into a rolling university of success.

Receive a **FREE AUDIO** of Pat Mesiti to help in getting you started!

FT THIS

TOUCH THIS

GET THIS

Your FREE special gifts from Pat Mesiti

**As a special reward for finishing this book,
I would like to take you to the next level.**

Claim these two very special offers by emailing
events@mesiti.com with your name, address and phone number.

Special Offer No.1
Receive **TWO FREE TICKETS** to ou
3 Day Wealth Creation Live Event
Valued at $997
Take your business, your relationship
and yourself to a whole new level!

Special Offer No.2
You've read the book and now yo
want to transform your car into
rolling university of success.

Receive a **FREE AUDIO** of Pat Mesi
to help in getting you started!

SHIFT THIS

TOUCH THIS

GET THIS

Pat Mesiti

Printed in the United States
By Bookmasters